ON BARBECUE

JOHN SHELTON REED

ON BARBECUE

The University of Tennessee Press
Knoxville

LIBRARY OF CONGRESS CATALOGING-IN-PUBLICATION DATA

Names: Reed, John Shelton, author. Title: On barbecue / John Shelton Reed.
Description: First edition. | Knoxville : The University of Tennessee Press, 2021. |
Includes bibliographical references and index. | Summary: "John Shelton Reed
compiles reviews, essays, magazine articles, op-eds, and book extracts from
his more than twenty-year obsession with the history and culture of barbecue.
Together these pieces constitute a broad look at the cultural, culinary,
historical, and social aspects of an American institution. A lover of tradition
whose study of regional distinctions has made him prize and defend them,
Reed writes with conviction on what 'real' barbecue looks, smells,
and tastes like. He delves into the history of barbecue and even the origins
of the word barbecue itself. Other topics include contemporary trends
in barbecue, Carolina 'cue and other regional varieties, and even
a couple of recipes"— Provided by publisher.
Identifiers: LCCN 2021001865 (print) | LCCN 2021001866 (ebook) |
ISBN 9781621906384 (paperback) | ISBN 9781621906391 (kindle edition) |
ISBN 9781621906407 (pdf)
Subjects: LCSH: Barbecuing—United States—History. |
Barbecuing—United States—Anecdotes.
Classification: LCC TX840.B3 R4454 2021 (print) |
LCC TX840.B3 (ebook) | DDC 641.7/60973—dc23
LC record available at https://lccn.loc.gov/2021001865
LC ebook record available at https://lccn.loc.gov/2021001866

★ ★ ★

To the memory of
Dale Volberg Reed,
coauthor of *Holy Smoke*
and my partner in every way
for sixty years

CONTENTS

PREFACE

I'm an East Tennessean, and it may seem odd that I have written so much and been so opinionated about barbecue. East Tennessee is, after all, a place regrettably deficient in barbecue tradition. In fact, I knew almost nothing about the subject until about 1960, when I visited my future wife and co-author Dale, then a student at Duke, and was introduced to wood-cooked whole-hog barbecue with a vinegar-based sauce at Turnage's in Durham. I loved North Carolina barbecue from the first bite. (It was like cigarettes, but I had to give those up.) Eastern style or Piedmont? I don't care. That's heresy in North Carolina, but remember, I'm from out of state.

Although it's sad that I had to wait so long to taste what my pal Dennis Rogers called "the Holy Grub," there is an upside to having grown up in a barbecue desert: I'm free to enjoy anyone's smoked meat without feeling disloyal. My career took me all over the South—Kentucky to Alabama, South Carolina to Kansas City; everywhere I made a point of eating the local barbecue. My sister lived in Memphis, so I feasted on dry ribs at the Rendezvous, Cornish hen at Cozy Corner, and barbecue spaghetti at The Bar-B-Q Shop. Now I have a daughter and a Texan son-in-law in Austin, so I regularly eat brisket and sausage out yonder, and since my wife and daughters sent me to Brisket Camp at Texas A&M for my birthday in 2018, I've cooked some damn good brisket myself, if I do say so.

So I've eaten a lot of barbecue over the years. Along the way I reviewed a couple of books about it; I was a judge at the Memphis in May competition and wrote about that; then the Southern Foodways Alliance asked me to talk about it at one of their meetings. Things got really serious when Dale and

I agreed to write a book for the University of North Carolina Press called *Holy Smoke: The Big Book of North Carolina Barbecue*. Writing that and promoting it was such fun that since it was published I haven't written about much else.

At some point I realized that my contributions to barbecultural studies might add up to a small book, so here I've collected those reviews and essays, magazine columns, newspaper op-eds, and journal articles, along with some extracts from my books. Nearly all have been published before; in fact, most have been *collected* before. But I suspect there are readers who might be interested in what I've written about barbecue who aren't interested in anything else I've written. This volume is for them.

I have tinkered a bit to eliminate repetition, but inevitably some remains. Also unavoidably, there is a disproportionate emphasis on the barbecue of North Carolina, which is where I live, after all. And I do have a lot of opinions, strong ones. Once upon a time I didn't know enough to have any; in fact, I actually wrote once that I'd never met a smoked hog I didn't like. But I have now. You don't have to agree with my opinions—people often disagree when it comes to barbecue—but I do hope you'll find something here to think about.

ON BARBECUE

BARBECUE PAST

THE HISTORY AND PRESENT STATE OF SOUTHERN BARBECUE

Some time ago the University of North Carolina Press began a series of cookbooks, each of which focused on a particular (excuse the expression) iconic Southern food—peaches, buttermilk, cornbread, and so forth. When they asked my wife and me if we'd write one on what may be *the* iconic Southern food, I said yes almost as quickly as Dale said no. I knew the world didn't need another barbecue cookbook—I owned a few dozen myself—but this series needed one.

I started that book by addressing some fundamental questions, like: Where have we come from? Where are we going? For that matter, where the hell are we? That seems a good way to start this one, too.

PEOPLE HAVE ALWAYS and almost everywhere known that low-and-slow cooking is a good way to handle tough or gnarly meat, but we first encounter something Southerners would recognize as barbecue in the West Indies in the 1500s, where native Indians and Spanish newcomers had begun cooking European hogs on a sort of wooden frame that the Indians had formerly used for a miscellany of rodents, reptiles, and fish. In the 1690s a Dominican missionary observed that the Indians served the meat with a splash of lime juice and hot peppers. The Indians called the frame something that the Spanish heard as "barbacoa," from which the English took the word "barbecue."

Very quickly the word—though not immediately the sauce—migrated to the English colonies on the eastern seaboard of North America, where *barbecuing* came to mean cooking meat more or less Caribbean style and

3

THE BARBECUE.

In antebellum Virginia. Illustration from *My Ride to the Barbecue;
or, Revolutionary reminiscences of the Old Dominion*, 1860.

big community *barbecues* continued a British hog-roast tradition. These occasions saw hogs, sheep, sides of beef, and many types of game—squirrels,
possums, in Maryland even turtles—cooked over barbecue pits (literally pits,
or trenches) full of live coals.

A young Virginian writing to a London friend in 1784 described a typical
eighteenth-century barbecue:

> It's a shoat & sometimes a Lamb or Mutton & indeed sometimes a Beef splitt
> into & stuck on spitts, & then they have a large Hole dugg in the ground where
> they have a number of Coals made of the Bark [?] of Trees, put in this Hole.
> & then they lay the Meat over that within about six inches of the Coals, &
> then they Keep basting it with Butter & Salt & Water & turning it every now
> and then, until it is done, we then dine under a large shady tree or an harbour
> made of green bushes, under which we have benches & seats to sit on when
> we dine sumptuously.

This sounds great if you get to sit under the "harbour"—less so, of course, if you're a slave on the digging and basting crew.

Barbecues were often just excuses to get together and eat, drink, dance, and gamble, but they were also used to mark occasions like homecomings, reunions, and political campaigns, and to celebrate all manner of things. When news of the Treaty of Paris reached New Bern, North Carolina, for instance, a visiting Spanish army officer reported, "There was a barbecue (a roast pig) and a barrel of rum, from which the leading officials and citizens of the region promiscuously ate and drank with the meanest and lowest kind of people, holding hands and drinking from the same cup. It is impossible to imagine, without seeing it, a more purely democratic gathering."

The one thing missing from colonial-era barbecue was supplied early in the nineteenth century when someone introduced the mainland to that lime

At the Atlanta Exposition, 1895. Photograph by B. W. Kilburn.

juice and pepper seasoning. Most likely it was slaves from the islands: the African influence on Southern cuisine (on Southern life, for that matter) has often been to make things spicier. A lemon juice version caught on quickly and spread; soon the lemon juice was supplemented or replaced by vinegar, more easily obtained in the temperate zone; and the result was a simple vinegar, pepper, and salt combination, perhaps with a secret pinch of this and dash of that, used to mop the cooking meat and sprinkled on the resulting barbecue to season it.

Up until the twentieth century, Americans everywhere cooked a variety of domestic animals and game over pits, and mopped and served the meat with some version of that hot-and-sour sauce. In time, however, the appropriate meat or meats and even what cuts to cook became matters of geographic variation, and then of local tradition. Since the middle of the twentieth century what's regarded in one place as the only real kind of barbecue might not even be recognized as barbecue in another.

There's also no agreement about what sauce to use, if any. More often than not, the once ubiquitous vinegar-and-pepper sauce has been replaced by something else. A fateful development occurred when the Centennial Exposition of 1876 in Philadelphia introduced America to bottled tomato ketchup. It was only a matter of time before someone tinkered with barbecue sauce.

Various combinations of meat and sauce now define several major barbecue regions and a great many microregions. The church of barbecue has splintered into many denominations and, as in the original Reformation, Germans had a lot to do with it.

In eastern North Carolina and the adjoining part of South Carolina, the word "barbecue" now means only pork, but otherwise barbecue is still pretty much what it has been for the last two hundred years: whole hogs cooked and served with the classic vinegar-and-pepper sauce.

As you head west across North Carolina these days, however, somewhere around the middle of the state the sauce gets redder and sweeter. (See pages 123–30) That's because around the time of the First World War a number of barbecue stand operators in the Lexington and Salisbury area—nearly all of them with German names—began adding their compatriot Mr. Heinz's ketchup to the classic vinegar-and-pepper sauce. They also started cooking pork shoulders instead of whole hogs and what they wound up with was a barbecue version of a traditional German dish.

The story is similar in South Carolina. Areas in the Piedmont where barbecue is now pork shoulder and the sauce includes a tincture of ketchup are

German surname in Holly Hill, South Carolina.

German surname in Taylor, Texas.

areas where Germans settled. Moreover, a swath of the state from Columbia in the middle to Charleston on the coast boasts a unique yellow, mustard-based sauce, and the names attached to restaurants that serve it and bottlers who sell it make it obvious that it's those Germans again.

Germans also figure in the Kentucky barbecue story, particularly in the area around Owensboro, where Catholic parish barbecues have preserved a mutton tradition that has disappeared almost everywhere else. Many of those Catholics are of German descent, and it's significant that many older patrons of the local barbecue restaurants prefer their mutton served with rye bread.

But nowhere is the German influence more obvious than in central Texas, where nineteenth-century German and Czech settlers started meat markets like those back home, selling fresh pork and beef and sausage, and smoking their leftovers in brick smokers with separate fireboxes, as they had done in Europe. Robb Walsh remarks that they must have been bemused when black migrant cotton pickers took their smoked meat for barbecue and started eating it on butcher paper with crackers and pickles, but that is how "the

From *Harper's Weekly*, 1887. Wood engraving from a sketch by Horace Bradley.

Vintage Memphis, founded in 1922.

old meat markets came to be considered the quintessential Texas barbecue joints—despite the fact that the German smoked meats and sausages they originally produced weren't really barbecue at all."

Those migrant workers brought their taste for smoked meat west from the Deep South, where yet another barbecue tradition had become established. This time there are no Germans in the ancestral woodpile: the barbecue of the old Cotton Belt is almost entirely an African American creation. Black slaves did most of the barbecuing on the old plantation, cooking whole hogs both for the Big House and for themselves. For whatever reason, perhaps because white folks were less likely to want the tough or bony parts, even transformed by low and slow cooking, shoulders and ribs became popular cuts in the black community, first as products of whole-hog cooking, but eventually as the stand-alone raw material for barbecue stands and restaurants. Until the 1900s Deep South barbecue was mopped and sauced with the Mother Sauce, and some outposts of tradition still do it that way, but for most places these days what goes on ribs and pulled pork shoulder is no longer vinegar with stuff in it, but ketchup with stuff in it—thick, red, and sweet (often *very* sweet).

Memphis barbecue exemplifies the Deep South style. With nearly 200 barbecue places listed in its yellow pages, Memphis is a major barbecue center, but it's also a big city, with the ethnic diversity that implies, and when the pork barbecue of the Deep South came to town it ran up against Italian

Greek-owned home of "dry ribs."

and Greek restaurateurs who added their own twists. The result was only-in-Memphis dishes like "barbecue pizza," pulled pork shoulder in spaghetti sauce, and "dry ribs," rubbed with oregano and thyme.

Finally, one other significant Southern barbecue tradition is a recent one. Kansas City's barbecue scene dates from a rib stand opened in 1908 by a newcomer from the Memphis area, and the Kansas City barbecue of today has clearly evolved from the Memphis style, with a few Texas licks thrown in. It mixes and matches all sorts of meats with a variety of sauces (the most

Kansas City classic (note gas pumps).

popular sweet and ketchupy, like a Deep South sauce) and over a hundred restaurants in the city now serve it.

This pick-your-meat, pick-your-sauce style may be the future. It's what you usually find in chain restaurants and in new independent restaurants wherever there is no local tradition to inoculate against it, and it's even beginning to overwhelm the defenses of those places that do have their own styles. Although America's barbecue landscape is still delightfully diverse—local traditions still reflect varying physical environments, farming practices, and historical settlement patterns—soon, perhaps, the barbecue landscape will be as uniform as it was in the nineteenth century and ketchupy sauces will be found everywhere.

Another possibility, though, is not uniformity but dizzying variety. Until recently barbecue hasn't been about innovation. Barbecue cooks have been like Orthodox icon painters: some were more accomplished than others, but what they produced was established by tradition. Self-expression has been thought uncalled-for; creativity has been unnecessary, if not actually undesirable. Lately, however, barbecue has begun to appear on the menus of surprisingly high-toned restaurants, places with wine lists and valet parking, where it's being cooked by actual *chefs* who just can't resist adding cheffy touches. The results often taste pretty good, but this trend is yet another reason to be concerned about the future of local barbecue traditions.

Barbecue has seldom been "home cooking." Before the appearance of stands that sold barbecue retail it was pretty much limited to community and institutional events because the process typically produced large quantities of cooked meat that required large numbers of eaters. Even after refrigeration made that less of a problem, most were content to leave barbecue to the professionals, just because it's not easy to cook. But if local barbecue traditions are to be preserved in days to come, it may be up to home cooks to do it.

THERE'S A WORD FOR IT:
THE ORIGINS OF "BARBECUE"

When three of us wrote a book called *Holy Smoke*, its subtitle was "The Big Book of North Carolina Barbecue." It could have been much bigger, though; in particular, there was much more to say about the history of the word "barbecue." So I said it in this article in the journal *Southern Cultures*.

WHAT COULD BE MORE Southern than barbecue? Even when entrepreneurs have taken the dish to other parts of the world, the names of their establishments pay tribute to the origins of their product, either explicitly (Memphis Championship Barbecue in Las Vegas, Memphis Minnie's in San Francisco, the Carolina Country Kitchen in Brooklyn, the Arkansas Café in London) or at least by implication (Jake and Earl's in Cambridge, Massachusetts, Daisy May's in Manhattan, Dixie's in Bellevue, Washington). Rivaled only by grits as the national dish of the South, barbecue would appear to be as Southern, as indigenous, as it comes.

For all that Southerners have made barbecue our own, however, the fact remains that this symbol of the South, like kudzu, is an import. The technique of cooking over hardwood coals or a low fire, or with smoke and indirect heat from hardwood, at a low temperature (about the boiling point of water) exists in a great many different cultures, and has from time immemorial: Europeans and Africans were both familiar with it before they arrived in the New World and found the native Indians doing it. The hogs and cattle that are the usual subjects of the enterprise were brought from Europe, as was the vinegar that goes into most sauces. The peppers that usually go in as well are a West Indian contribution. And tomatoes—well, that's a long story, but let's just say that they weren't grown and eaten in colonial North America.

Even the word *barbecue* seems to have been imported (although it underwent some changes after it was naturalized in Great Britain's North American colonies). The word came into English only some five hundred years ago. In the first decades of the 1500s Spanish explorers in the Caribbean found the locals using frameworks of sticks to support meat over fires. They did this either to slow-cook it or to cure and preserve it (as we do with country hams and jerky today)—which one depends on the heat of the fire and the height of the framework. Both on the island of Hispaniola (Haiti and the Dominican Republic today) and on the northern coast of South America, this apparatus was called something that the Spanish heard as *barbacòa*, which soon became a Spanish word (one that is making its way into the South these days, via Mexico). A French expedition to Florida in the 1560s included an artist, Jacques Le Moyne, one of whose sketches of Timucua Indian life shows a mixed grill of alligators, snakes, and some kind of wildcat on just such a frame. The Native Floridians also had a word like barbacòa for this rig, and indeed for all sorts of wooden structures, including watchtowers and raised sleeping platforms.

Florida Indians with a barbacoa, ca. 1562. Drawing by Jacques Le Moyne.

Some twenty years later, in 1585, Sir Walter Raleigh sent some folks to look things over on the coast of what would later be North Carolina. One member of that party was John White, "Gentleman of London," who later became governor of the ill-fated Roanoke Island colony (and grandfather of Virginia Dare who was, as every North Carolina schoolchild once knew, the first English child born in North America). White made sketches of what he saw, including Croatan Indians "broyling their fishe over the flame—they took great heed that they bee not burntt." Unfortunately, he didn't say what the indigenous Tar Heels called their cooker, but whatever they called it, it's obviously a barbacòa, too.

William Dampier, naturalist and sometime pirate, wrote in 1697 about a visit to some West Indians when he and his companions "lay there all night, upon our Borbecu's, or frames of Sticks, raised about 3 foot from the Ground." Yankees and Australians who talk about putting meat "on the barbecue" can appeal to Dampier for precedent, but in colonial North America and England, as in the South today, the word usually referred to a process of cooking or to what was cooked, rather than to the frame on which it was done.

The earliest use of the English word that I've encountered comes from 1661, when Edmund Hickeringill's *Jamaica Viewed* reported that animals

"Barbicu" in 1688.

"are slain, And their flesh forthwith Barbacu'd and eat," but by 1688 in a play called *The Widdow Ranter, or, the History of Bacon in Virginia*, "the rabble" fixing to lynch one Colonel Wellman cry, "Let's barbicu this fat rogue." That the word could be used casually on the stage shows that by then it must have been familiar to London audiences. (The play was written by the remarkable Aphra Behn, the first Englishwoman to be a professional writer, and "Bacon" in the title refers to the leader of Bacon's Rebellion of 1676, not to side meat.) About the same time, the Boston Puritan Cotton Mather used the word in the same gruesome sense when he reported that several hundred Narragansetts slaughtered by New England troops in 1675 (among them women, children, and elders burned in their lodges) had been "terribly Barbikew'd."

A few years later John Lawson, surveyor-general of North Carolina, also used the word without explanation. In his *New Voyage to Carolina* (1709) Lawson encountered "barbakued"—that is, smoked and dried—venison, fish, and even peaches. Some Santee Indians served him "fat barbacu'd Venison" that sounds like a sort of jerky: "The Woman of the Cabin took [it] and tore in Pieces with her Teeth, so put it into a Mortar, beating it into Rags," then boiled it. But he was also served "roasted or barbakued Turkey, eaten with Bears Fat." Not long after that, the physician and naturalist John Brickell gave a very similar account (so similar in fact that it may have been plagiarized) in his *Natural History of North Carolina* (1737).

The one suggestion I've found that the English word was not taken from the Spanish version of a Caribbean Indian word comes from Robert Beverley's *History and Present State of Virginia* (1705). Beverley reported that the Indians of the Carolinas and Virginia had "two ways of Broyling viz. one by laying the Meat itself upon the Coals, the other by laying it upon Sticks rais'd upon Forks at some distance above the live Coals, which heats more gently, and drys up the Gravy," and added, "this [latter] they, and we also from them, call Barbacueing." (Whether they had the same word as their Caribbean cousins or not, they plainly got the grilling versus barbecuing thing.)

The English may have copied the Indians' vocabulary, but they didn't feel constrained to copy their Stone Age gear. Anglo-Saxons and Celts had been roasting meat for a few thousand years themselves, and had made a few improvements in the matter of cooking frames. In 1732 Richard Bradley gave directions in *The Country House-wife* for "an Hog barbecued": "Take a large Grid-iron, with two or three Ribs in it, and set it upon a stand of iron, about three Foot and a half high, and upon that, lay your Hog . . . Belly-side downwards." And a 1744 advertisement in the *Boston News-Letter* offered for sale "a Lusty Negro Man, works well at the Smith's Trade; likewise a Grate for to burn Coal; a large Gridiron, fit for a large Kitchen, or a Barbeque." (It also offers the earliest example I've found of the *-que* spelling, although spelling was so random at the time that it hardly signifies.)

Still, the process of cooking or smoking meat on some sort of frame remained identified with the Indians. When Colonel George Washington, trying to get provisions for his troops during the French and Indian War, wrote his superior officer in 1758, "We have not an ounce of salt provision of any kind here; and it is impossible to preserve the fresh (especially as we have no Salt) by any other means than barbacuing it in the indian manner," he was evidently writing about smoking meat to cure it, not to cook it. Later, however, the future Father of His Country often wrote about going to "barbecues" where cooking was the object: for example, "Went in to Alexandria to a Barbecue and stayed all Night" (1769), "Went to a Barbicue of my own giving at Accotinck" (1773), "Went to the Barbacue at Accatinck" (1774). (Notice that his spelling was as independent as his subsequent politics.)

Washington's use of *barbecue* to refer to a social event was not unusual: That use of the word dates from at least 1733, although it was apparently an Americanism. When a young Virginian wrote to a London friend in 1784 that he was "continually at Balls & Barbecues," he added, "the latter I don't suppose you know what I mean" and went on to explain.

This sort of event was probably the kind of thing the itinerant Anglican parson Charles Woodmason smelled, roaming the South Carolina backcountry in 1768, when he wrote in his journal: "I had last Week Experience of the Velocity and force of the Air—By smelling a Barbicu dressing in the Woods upwards of six Miles."

Even though the word had been naturalized in the thirteen colonies, the British continued to see it as West Indian. Also, most references at this time were to whole hogs (or whole other animals) being cooked—the practice in the Caribbean and, now as then, in eastern North Carolina. When the poet Alexander Pope wrote in 1733 that a man named Oldfield, who was famous for his appetite, "cries, 'Send me, Gods! a whole Hog barbecu'd!'" he added a note for his English readers explaining that "a whole hog barbecu'd" was "a West-Indian Term of Gluttony, a Hog roasted whole, stu'd with Spice, and basted with Madera Wine." Just so, Samuel Johnson's famous *Dictionary* (1755) defined the verb *to barbecue* as "a term used in the West-Indies for dressing a hog whole; which, being split to the backbone, is laid flat upon a large gridiron, raised about two feet above a charcoal fire, with which it is surrounded" and *barbecue*, the noun, as "a hog drest whole in the West Indian manner." Virtually identical definitions, probably cribbed from Johnson, can be found

Nineteenth-century ox roast.

in many, many subsequent dictionaries. In 1828 Noah Webster's *Dictionary of the American Language* also defined the word as, "In the West Indies, a hog roasted whole," but expanded the definition: "It is, with us [i.e., Americans], used for an ox or perhaps any other animal dressed in like manner."

Webster was from Connecticut, but an 1816 *Vocabulary, or, Collection of words and phrases, which have been supposed to be peculiar to the United States of America* [etc.] had given the first indication that barbecue was becoming a Southern thing. Quoting an English source from 1798, it said that barbecue was "a porket . . . stuffed with spices and other rich ingredients, and basted with Madeira wine," then added, "Used in the Southern states" (although "not peculiar to the United States; it is used in the West Indies also").

Notice that these dictionaries show the emergence of yet another use of this versatile word: a barbecue could mean the critter being cooked. And not just a hog; in 1796 Hugh Henry Brackenridge wrote a humorous reply to a challenge to duel, which read in part, "I do not see any good it would do me to put a bullet through any part of your body. . . . You might make a good barbecue, it is true, being of the nature of a raccoon or an opossum; but people are not in the habit of barbecuing anything human now."

Turning the meat at the 1895 Atlanta Exposition. Drawing by W. A. Rogers.

So by the mid-1700s we had barbecue as a kind of equipment for a style of cooking called barbecuing, we had barbecue as an event of the sort that George Washington and his contemporaries went to, and we had barbecue as a word for the subject of the undertaking—pig, ox, shad, whatever (although this last use seems to have disappeared). But we apparently did not yet have barbecue as the point of all this: the dish prepared on a barbecue-device and served at a barbecue-event, what a barbecue-creature becomes after it is barbecue-processed. When did barbecued pork become pork barbecue?

Someone may come up with an earlier example, but the earliest I've found comes from 1808. Oddly enough, it comes from a Yankee—although he was disparaging Southern folkways at the time. In a speech on the floor of Congress, Representative Josiah Quincy of Boston denounced the kind of partisan stump speech commonly delivered "in this quarter of the country ... while the gin circulated, while barbecue was roasting." (It was a Southern thing. He didn't understand.) By the middle of the nineteenth century this use of the word was increasingly common in print, especially in Southern newspapers, usually in the context of political rallies. In 1859, for instance, the *Weekly Standard* of Raleigh wrote that one politician's "constituents had been bought up by whiskey and barbecue." In 1868 the *Petersburg Index* reported that the three thousand Democrats at a rally in Nash County, North Carolina, "marched to the grove, near by, where a bountiful supply of barbecue, vegetables, etc., etc., refreshed the 'inner man,' and to which ample justice was done."

True, as late as 1894, when the *Statesville* (North Carolina) *Landmark* wrote of an occasion where "several hundred ladies were present, and the contents of their baskets, supplemented by 'barbecue' from the committee, composed the repast," the paper put the noun in quotation marks, suggesting that the usage remained colloquial. Still, by then everyone seems to have known that it meant something you could put on a plate or a sandwich.

Once that was understood, Southerners could begin the eternal argument about what barbecue *is*.

BARBECUE IN THE
HEART OF DIXIE

Barbecue differs from place to place, so there is a large and growing library of books about the multifarious barbecue of individual cities and states (see pages 159–60). This is a review of the one about Alabama.

IN THE 1820s, some citizens of Madison County, Alabama, grew concerned about the bad effects of public barbecues on manners, morals, and the quality of political candidates. A writer who called himself "Barbecuensis" claimed that they were scenes of "unbounded license" where even "slavery forgot its chain, and the tawny sons of Africa danced, sung, and balloed [*sic*]." The reformers called on Alabamians to "turn at last from shote and grog" and "act the man, and not the hog."

Their efforts were unavailing. Despite an anti-barbecue petition signed by more than a thousand people, candidates continued to woo voters with "fiddling, feasting, dancing, drinking, masquing / And other things which may be had for asking" until the 1840s, when the Whigs began to encourage women to attend. Eventually the presence of ladies had a calming effect, and in time barbecues became respectable, even genteel. By 1897 the Barbour County United Daughters of the Confederacy were holding them to raise funds for a Confederate monument.

This is just one of many stories that Mark A. Johnson shares with us in his book, *An Irresistible History of Alabama Barbecue: From Wood Pit to White Sauce*. (Since no one style defines the state, perhaps one should say "barbecue in Alabama," not "Alabama barbecue," but let's not get picky.)

Famous Tuscaloosa rib joint.

The first section brings the story up to the end of the nineteenth century. Until then barbecue was a matter of cooking whole animals over live coals, outside, to feed large groups. But with the coming of the automobile came the rise of the barbecue restaurant. Johnson discusses the origins and pro-liferation of that institution and examines more than a dozen of the three hundred or so in the state—places like Brenda's in Montgomery, Lannie's in Selma, Archibald's in Northport, Whitt's in Athens, the Golden Rule in Irondale, and the Green Top in Dora—often as interesting for their histories as for their food.

This is not a guidebook, but it sounds as if all at least "*mérite un détour*," as the Michelin guide used to say of its two-star establishments. In fact, as a sometime barbecue pilgrim from out-of-state, I think two of them deserve three stars ("*vaut le voyage*"). One is the original Dreamland in Tuscaloosa (not the anodyne branches elsewhere), where it's all about the ribs, served with the sauce that the Lord gave to John "Big Daddy" Bishop in a dream sixty years ago, white bread that doubles as a napkin—and nothing else. The other is Big Bob Gibson's in Decatur (the 6th Avenue location, with the dancing neon pig). In 1925 Big Bob started dunking his barbecued chicken in the mayonnaise-based "white sauce" of Johnson's subtitle, the sauce caught on, and the Tennessee River valley is now a widely recognized barbecue microregion.

There is much, ah, food for thought here. It's striking, for instance, that lo-cal barbecue joints have played a role both in the effort to preserve segregation

Origin of Alabama white sauce.

(Ollie's in Birmingham figured in the 1964 *Katzenbach v. McClung* decision) and in the effort to end it (Lannie's in Selma fed civil-rights workers at the height of the movement). Johnson's examples also illustrate the importance of Greek-American restaurateurs in the world of barbecue, a connection not unique to Alabama, but perhaps more obvious there than elsewhere.

The book is copiously illustrated with marvelous photographs, historical and contemporary (many of the latter in color). The earlier ones are mostly of buildings and people, both often on the funky side, while the recent ones are mostly of food. It seems that barbecue places aren't as picturesque as they once were, and there's a reason for that. Since the golden age of vernacular barbecue restaurants in the mid-twentieth century, Johnson shows, the business has moved away from locally owned, independent barbecue places (many also beer joints). These days, as often as not, Alabamians eat barbecue cooked on a gas or electric cooker with a smoke box, at a branch of a chain restaurant which offers an extended menu including out-of-state specialties like beef brisket.

Some of these chains are old places that have opened branches—Dreamland, for instance, with ten, or Whitt's, with over thirty in three states—but in a chapter titled "Barbecue and Beyond—Alabama Barbecue Restaurants in the Twenty-First Century" Johnson looks at three new enterprises probably meant from the start to be chains. Saw's BBQ, a newcomer established in 2009 in Homewood, is now on its way with two other locations and a food truck, while Jim 'N Nick's Community Bar-B-Q, founded by father and son Jim and Nick Pihakis in Birmingham in 1985, and Moe's Original Bar B Que, started by three University of Alabama graduates in Vail, Colorado, in 2001, have both become major interstate players: Jim 'N Nick's now has sixteen locations in Alabama and a couple of dozen more in six other states, while Moe's has metastasized to twenty branches in Alabama and more than forty others in fifteen other states and Mexico. (By the way, "Moe" was a Tuscaloosa pitmaster, Moses Day, from whom the owners of Moe's say they learned their craft.)

Rousseau observed that man, born free, is now found everywhere in chains, and this is probably the future of barbecue (not just in Alabama). Johnson's book ends, though, with a chapter on the barbecue clubs of West

Founded in Vail, Colorado.

Alabama, which are in many ways a throwback. Clubs that met regularly to eat barbecue were once widespread in the South and some antebellum examples still survive in South Carolina. In Alabama, however, new clubs were being started well into the twentieth century, and today there are at least seven in Sumter County alone, one of which (Timilichee) still cooks whole hogs. Gump Ozment of the Sumterville club observes, "In the country, the only time you see folks is when you go to church, go to a funeral, or go to a barbecue club," and the clubs apparently do serve the same social functions as the community barbecues of the nineteenth century. The food's pretty good, too.

The audience for this book—well, let's put it this way: Alabamians ought to read it. People anywhere who care about barbecue should read it, too. Alabamians who care about barbecue ought to *own* it.

KENTUCKY 'CUE

When Kentucky is mentioned at all in accounts of American barbecue, it is usually just a passing reference to the quirky mutton tradition of Daviess County. I confess that I've done that myself. But the book reviewed here persuades me that the Bluegrass State deserves more attention and more respect.

WES BERRY, a professor of English at Western Kentucky University, has written a valuable guidebook for culinary tourists. Next time I go to Kentucky, I hope to have a copy of his *Kentucky Barbecue Book* in my glove compartment.

But this is far more than a guidebook. It is a splendid piece of Kentuckiana, and it also has the ingredients for a wonderful stand-alone essay on barbecue geography and the extremely local nature of barbecue and side dishes. Berry's discussion of "the mutton line," his delineation of various microregions (for smoked city ham or sliced pork butt, for instance), his spotting of "alien" barbecue brought in from Texas and Florida, his pondering of the west-to-east gradient and the virtual absence of barbecue restaurants in Appalachia—all of these topics cry out for further investigation.

Berry also makes a strong case for treating Kentucky (at least western and central Kentucky) as a major barbecue region in its own right, the peer of the Carolinas, Memphis, Texas, and Kansas City. Any reading of the historical record would put nineteenth-century Kentucky right in the center of America's barbecue heartland—I've seen at least a dozen accounts of grand political and civic barbecues in the state—but somehow in the twentieth

The Great G.A.R. Encampment, Louisville, 1895.

Gus Jaubert, late-nineteenth-century Kentucky pitmaster.

century Kentucky slipped off the radar. Berry makes it clear that this was not because Kentuckians stopped barbecuing (as Virginians pretty much did), and that a tradition persists, worthy of attention and respect, and with its own unique features. Kentuckians will apparently barbecue almost anything, for instance, but some have clung to mutton, largely abandoned elsewhere.

A mutton barbecue place in Owensboro, Kentucky.

Outside Kentucky I've only encountered corn cakes with barbecue in Middle Tennessee, and that was probably spillover. In parts of Kentucky, as in other conservative locales like eastern North Carolina and northern Arkansas, the sauce or "dip" is still the nineteenth-century "mother sauce" of vinegar, cayenne, and salt, but Kentuckians add the lard or butter that is no longer used anywhere else I know of. By the way, after reading this I think present-day Kentucky may have more old-fashioned wood-cooking barbecue establishments than North Carolina, if not Texas. God bless Kentucky, I say.

Finally, Berry has written a love letter to the old Kentucky. He writes from the heart, and used his barbecue quest as an excuse to get off the interstates and to savor the landscapes and people found along the blue highways and country roads of his state. He is wise to let so many Kentuckians speak for themselves, in their own voices. I'm not a Kentuckian myself, but reading this book almost made me wish I were.

Not everyone will like this book. When it comes to smoke, and sauce, and texture, and degree of doneness, Berry has opinions and doesn't hesitate to share them—although when he's being critical he usually tries to find something nice to say as well. For my part, I find his opinions well-informed and well-expressed. Perhaps his book will serve to educate some of those people living in darkness who think riblets at Applebee's are barbecue.

DOES EAST TENNESSEE
HAVE A BARBECUE TRADITION?

In an early draft of this book's preface I offhandedly asserted that East Tennessee, the place of my childhood and youth, has "no real barbecue tradition." That was certainly my impression growing up there, and it has been shared by some otherwise well-informed observers. But it seems that I was guilty at least of overstatement. I'm happy to correct the record.

JOE DABNEY, the author of *Smokehouse Ham, Spoon Bread, and Scuppernong Wine: The Folklore and Art of Southern Appalachian Cooking,* once wrote, "I can't figure out why mountain folks never turned to barbecuing. It's a mystery, come to think about it. Lord knows they killed enough hogs, and got everything from the porkers except the squeal." But he said that, for whatever reason, "my research for 'Smokehouse' didn't turn up much barbecuing in the mountains of North Carolina or Tennessee."

That sounded right to me, and I blithely echoed Joe's observation for years. But when I put it in print, for the preface to this book, my fellow East Tennessean Fred Sauceman challenged it. Since Fred has written a few books about Appalachian cuisine himself, I thought I'd better look into it.

It seems that, historically, special-occasion community barbecues were not uncommon in East Tennessee and adjoining parts of Virginia and North Carolina, though perhaps less frequent than in the flatlands. In 1923, for instance, the *Kingsport Times* reported three in its coverage area: two in Kingsport held by the "Central Baptist Church (colored)" and a fundraiser to build a swimming pool at Martha Washington College in Abingdon, Virginia.

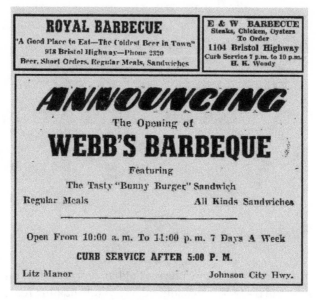

From the *Kingsport News*, 1943–1946.

The practice continued through midcentury, with at least a couple of dozen reported by the *Kingsport News* in the twenty years after World War II. Many of these were in support of political candidates, evenly divided between Democratic and Republican, and politicians showed up at other events as well. In 1950, for instance, a combination barbecue and real estate auction in Dandridge promised "Speaking by Congressman and Candidates for Senate," and a 1953 fundraiser for Kingswood School offered meat prepared by Minnis Brown of Greeneville, "a barbecue specialist," and the oratory of Governor Frank Clement. Barbecues also accompanied college homecomings and county Farm Bureau meetings. They were sponsored by a rod and gun club, a bankers' association, an American Legion post, and the Lonesome Pine Country Club in Big Stone Gap. They celebrated the openings of a high school in Rye Cove and a tobacco warehouse in Weber City (the latter with an address by Robert Porterfield of the Barter Theatre in Abingdon, Virginia).

Some of these events drew enormous crowds—"500 families" at one Sullivan County Farm Bureau annual meeting; "over a thousand" at another—and they seem to have been easygoing about what sort of meat to serve. A farm auction offered "barbecue pork and beef," along with "plenty of hillbilly music." A group preparing for a Farm Bureau meeting had procured "a steer and 1500 pounds of charcoal." Borden Mills held a barbecue for its fifteen hundred employees and their families featuring "beef, pork, and mutton," cooked on a seventy-five-foot pit.

But for some reason the community barbecue tradition didn't make the transition to barbecue stands and restaurants the way it did elsewhere in the South. In the 1940s and early 1950s a few advertisements and stories in the *Kingsport News* mention what sound like barbecue stands, but they seem to have had a hard time making it on barbecue alone. In Kingsport a half-dozen advertisers had the word "barbecue" in their name, but their advertisements mention everything *except* barbecue. E&W Barbecue's "clean wholesome food," for example, included "Steak, French Fries, and Salad," "Chicken Dinners," and "Plate Lunches," then (after a change in management) a specialty of "Home-Made Chili," then (after another change) "Steaks, Chicken, and Oysters to Order." The house special at Webb's Barbecue was "the Tasty 'Bunny Burger' Sandwich." The Royal Barbecue, managed by Najim Izzeddin, advertised only "The Coldest Beer in Town" and "Short Orders, Regular Meals, Sandwiches."

In other words, just because a place was called Somebody's Barbecue doesn't mean it was a barbecue place, as that phrase is understood in, say, Texas, Memphis, Alabama, or North Carolina. Most were or became conventional plate lunch or sandwich places, or drive-ins; others that seem to have been primarily beer joints closed when Sullivan County went dry in 1952.

In the 1950s a couple of proper barbecue restaurants opened in Kingsport, but they didn't last. A newspaper account from 1953 is worth quoting at length:

The Beacon Drive-In Restaurant held its grand opening Monday for some 2000 guests who were introduced to manager "Big Jim" Williams' barbecued ham, coleslaw and hush puppies straight out of about the most modern and largest barbecue pit in the South.

Red hot hickory fired away in the oven and the hot coals raked under the barbecue racks sizzled 10- to 12-pound-sized hams to a rich velvet brown. Potential customers, filing through the pit and seeing the actual barbecuing were each given a tray to sample. The pit is large enough to barbecue 50 hams or 500 pounds of beef at once.

Owner Bill Harrell said the drive-in barbecue will specialize in trays of sliced and chopped barbecue meat—beef, pork, and chicken.

Clearly the original Beacon was a real barbecue place, but by the time my buddies and I were cruising it five or six years later it had become a generic

From the *Kingsport News*, 1953.

teen hangout, with burgers and hot dogs; I don't recall the pit building and if they still served barbecue it wasn't a big deal.

In fact, when the Smoke House opened in 1956 it billed itself as "Kingsport's only real barbecue restaurant," implying that the Beacon was no longer one. The Smoke House may not have actually been one itself. Its "Opening Special" was a turkey dinner "with all the trimmings," and although it served "Pit Barbecue (Beef and Pork) and Hushpuppies," it also advertised country ham and biscuits, T-bone steaks, and "free coffee & cinnamon rolls all day Thursday." In any case, it didn't last long either.

These days there are some barbecue restaurants in East Tennessee and elsewhere in Appalachia—even a famous one, the Ridgewood in Bluff City—but unlike eastern North Carolina, where barbecue restaurants essentially brought the community barbecue indoors, or the North Carolina Piedmont, where you can trace a family tree of master-apprentice links from the Lexington pioneers, mountain establishments tend to be the fruits of individual entrepreneurs who brought in outside traditions or made it up as they went along.

Consider the sauces they use. In *The Place Setting*, Fred Sauceman discusses four barbecue places with dramatically different offerings. At the Ridgewood, the Proffitt family started selling barbecue in the 1950s after they ran into it on a trip to Daytona, and they devised their own remarkable Kansas City-style sauce to go with it (see page 151). At Broad Street Barbecue

Ridgewood Barbecue sign, Bluff City, Tennessee (note bullet holes).

in Kingsport, the owner learned to cook barbecue from a friend in West Tennessee and serves it with a Memphis-style ketchup and molasses sauce. Mike's, in Mountain City, serves a unique nineteen-ingredient sauce invented by its founder, a "self-taught pitmaster." The Dixie BBQ, in Johnson City, has closed, but it offered a sauce smorgasbord: thick and sweet, vinegar and pepper, mustard-based South Carolina-style, mayonnaise-based Alabama "white," and something called the "Sauce from Hell." To Sauceman's list one could add 12 Bones, in nearby Asheville, which has won a *Good Morning America* prize for its blueberry-chipotle rib sauce, one of so many sauces and rubs offered that they rotate the choices.

This independent streak extends to what is cooked. Many places offer beef or cook unusual cuts of pork. Tommy Monk of Lexington Barbecue says that, like nearly all places in piedmont North Carolina, "We only use the shoulder. Someone else has a whole lot of hams." Well, that "somebody else" might be the Ridgewood, which cooks *only* hams (like Kingsport's Beacon Drive-In when it was a barbecue place). Across the border in North Carolina, Herb's Barbecue, in Murphy, cooks loins and collars.

I'm now convinced that I was wrong to write that East Tennessee has "no real barbecue tradition," but it's fair to say that it has no real tradition of barbecue *restaurants*, and that what restaurants exist now don't adhere to any local tradition. So I've changed what I wrote to say that East Tennessee is merely "regrettably deficient" in barbecue tradition.

The question remains why that is so, and, as Joe Dabney said, that is a mystery.

BARBECUE AND THE
SOUTHERN PSYCHE

> Barbecue can be treated seriously, but it shouldn't be treated solemnly. The book reviewed here certainly doesn't do that. There aren't many books I wish I'd written, but this is one of them.

WILBER "PETE" CALDWELL, who lives in Gilmer County, Georgia, has written on subjects as diverse as public architecture and cynicism. Now, in *Searching for the Dixie Barbecue: Journeys into the Southern Psyche*, he turns his attention to barbecue, and he obviously had a really good time writing this book.

He begins with a brief essay on the history of pit-cooked meat from Prometheus onward, but concludes that barbecue is an American—specifically, a Southern—invention, if only because most Southerners believe that barbecue isn't barbecue if it's not *called* barbecue. Bringing in Prometheus (and the *Iliad*, and Brillat-Savarin) reveals his learning—worn lightly, thank goodness, since nothing could be more dreary than a pedantic treatment of this subject except maybe a postmodern one. (In one instance, alas, the learning is deployed carelessly: "Harleian" is not the writer of a medieval cookbook but the name of the British Library collection that includes it.) (I'm just showing off.)

Caldwell moves on to a series of loosely connected chapters that answer a great many fascinating questions that it hadn't occurred to me to ask. For instance:

- * how barbecue manners differ from regular table manners, and when each is appropriate
- * how three places in the same county can all have "the best barbecue in [the county/the state/the South/the nation/the world]," and what "world famous" might mean in that context
- * why some Southerners don't like Brunswick stew (because it reminds them of school cafeteria food)
- * why side dishes are generally boring (because they are "designed not to distract from the main event")
- * what Southerners usually tell the truth about (e.g., war records, athletic achievements) and what they feel free to lie about because everyone knows they're lying (e.g., fishing, barbecue)
- * why everyone, black and white, knows that black barbecue and white barbecue are different, despite the fact that they're apparently not
- * how "never" and "generally not" are used (as in the rule that one never serves cornbread with barbecue, except when one is serving greens with the barbecue, but one does not generally

The Red Pig in Concord, North Carolina.

serve greens with barbecue), and what that tells us about
Southern thought

In this last example I have paraphrased to avoid Caldwell's phonetic rendition of Southern speech, an uncharacteristic misstep which sometimes lends an unfortunate Simon Suggs flavor to the proceedings. In general, however, he has a good ear; it lets him have fun, for example, with the names people give to barbecue sauces. He offers some of his own, like "Piney Woods Wilber's 'Let the Big Dog Eat' Georgia BBQ Sauce," and even gives the recipe for one with a name not family-friendly that starts with a gallon each of ketchup and vinegar and winds up with a quart of 10W-30 motor oil and "Clorox Brand Bleach as needed."

Caldwell savors places like the late Red Pig Barbecue in Concord, North Carolina, which used to sport its "C" health rating as a badge of honor, and he offers a useful index for calculating an establishment's "funk factor," with a base score for architectural features (e.g., +10 for no windows), adjusted for various add-ons and deductions (e.g., minus ½ point for designated handicapped parking; plus ½ point for plastic flowers, displays of firearms,

Columbus, Georgia, near Fort Benning (Farm Security Administration photo by Marion Post Wolcott, ca. 1940).

or pictures of Jesus; minus one full point if the place has a website). This doesn't just work for barbecue joints, by the way. Before my all-time favorite oyster shack in South Carolina was rebuilt after a fire, it had a damn near perfect score.

This is not all fun and games, however. Caldwell has actually done some serious (well, sort of serious) research. He reports, for example, on a survey of the side dishes served by fifty establishments. (He doesn't consider Brunswick stew a side dish: It gets its own chapter.) Nearly all serve the "holy trinity" of coleslaw, baked beans, and potato salad. Potato chips, french fries, and hushpuppies follow at a considerable distance, with corn on the cob far behind, and nothing else served by more than a handful of the places.

If there seems to be a consensus on what should be served with barbecue, let me add, in the same empirical spirit, that Caldwell's photographs reveal an encouraging independence when it comes to spelling. Only four of the sixty-six signs displayed spell the word "barbecue" that way: fully half prefer "Bar-B-Q," another quarter go with "BBQ," and "Bar-B-Que" is also popular.

By the way, there are ninety-some of those photographs, and they would make a good coffee-table book in their own right. Most show places in the top quartile of funkiness, and a few are off the scale. I'm happy to report that three-quarters are from Georgia, which means there's still a lot of "research" left for those of us from other states.

**BARBECUE PRESENT
AND YET TO COME**

THANK YOU FOR SMOKING

The first book I know that took barbecue seriously was published in 1988, and this review of it is the first piece I ever wrote about barbecue. There have been some changes since then, of course. I'm reliably informed that Wild Horse Mountain BBQ has a health certificate, for instance; more importantly, many places the book mentions have closed. The authors couldn't have known at the time, nor did I, that locally owned community barbecue establishments were endangered, but now . . . Brother Jack's, Allen & Son, OT's, Harold's, the Auburn Avenue Rib Shack, Scruggs's—all are gone.

A WISE MAN once observed that the existence of a nation requires that a great many things be forgotten—in particular, those things that divide its people. Maybe that's why the South never made it as an independent state.

Black and white Southerners have had their disagreements in the past, of course, and so have flatlanders and hillbillies, rednecks and gentry. Politics and religion have usually been at least as good for an argument here as anywhere else. And right up there in divisive potential is barbecue.

In this respect (others, too, of course) barbecue is unlike grits. Grits glue the South together, if you'll excuse the image. Black and white, uplands and lowlands, everybody likes grits. A number of years ago, a fellow named Stan Woodward made a marvelous movie called *It's Grits*, an hour or so of heartwarming grits lore, with testimonials from illustrious Southerners like Strom Thurmond and Craig Claiborne and from common folk including the entire crowd at a South Carolina Gamecocks football game ("Give me a G! Give me an R!"). The last time I saw Stan, though, he was starting to film a movie on barbecue, and he hasn't been heard from since. I'm afraid he's a casualty. Reporting Southern barbecue is like reporting Lebanon: risky business.

Smoked meat is a subject folks can get excited about, you know what I mean? Barbecue drives a wedge between Texas (beef) and the Carolinas (pork), and completely isolates those parts of Kentucky around Owensboro (mutton). Even porcivores can't agree: barbecue divides western North Carolina (tomato) from eastern North Carolina (no tomato), not to mention from

Overlooked by the Pulitzer Prize Board, 1988.

South Carolina (mustard). You might say barbecue pits Southerners against one another. (Sorry.)

Now, personally, I don't regret these hard feelings. If they keep the South's proud local barbecue traditions alive—well, long may they wave. When a "Texas-style" barbecue restaurant opened in my Carolina hometown, I was delighted to see it go out of business within a year. Not that I don't like brisket: I love it, in Texas. But eating that stuff here was like drinking Dr Pepper in Munich—just not *right*, you understand?

Southern barbecue is the closest thing we Americans have to Europe's wines or cheeses; drive a hundred miles and the barbecue changes. Let's keep it that way.

Anyone who cares about barbecue needs to see a savory book by Greg Johnson and Vince Staten, called *Real Barbecue*. This is one important book, a cultural landmark. Remember a movie called *The Endless Summer*? This book does with barbecue what that did with surfing. Johnson and Staten are reporters in Louisville, and they are fanatics. They are, in other words, just the men to travel forty thousand miles and eat roughly two hundred pounds of barbecue (629,200 calories) in order to compile a sort of *Whole Barbecue Catalog*: 260 pages, with annotated listings of barbecue joints, sources for flash-frozen air freight barbecue, recipes for side dishes, and plans for monster cookers guaranteed to capture your neighbors' attention. Boxed here and there are some tasty barbecue quotations (although not the raunchy testimonial from the North Carolina-born novelist Tom Robbins that the prurient can find on page 57 of *Another Roadside Attraction*). The book also includes nice little essays on such topics as the names of barbecue joints—"Bubba's" is indeed a favorite—and why Cincinnati doesn't have good barbecue.

Inevitably, the book has a Southern slant, since nearly all of the great pit-folk come from the South, and most are still in it. But Greg and Vince have worked real hard to include the rest of the country. Maybe too hard: Their affirmative action has turned up what they claim is semi-decent barbecue in Vermont and a mail-order sauce from Castro Street, San Francisco. When I know what these guys are talking about, though, they do have pretty close to perfect pitch (I'd thought the fact that O'Brien's in Rockville was actually good was my very own secret discovery), so I want to try some of the places I don't know. As a matter of fact, I was reading the book while visiting Chicago, and tried to promote an excursion to Lem's or Leon's for some South Side ribs, but my quiche-eating Hyde Park hosts thought I was out of my mind. Next time.

I do confess to mixed feelings about the book's list of great joints, because

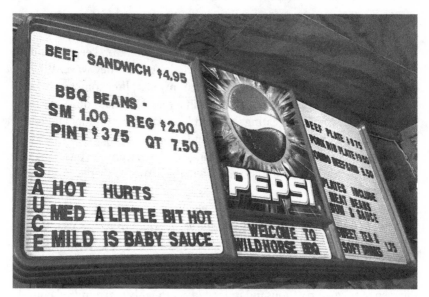

On the wall at the Wild Horse Mountain Bar-B-Que, Sallisaw, Oklahoma.

Famous South Side Chicago rib joint, founded in 1954.

it's almost a law that fame isn't good for such places. As Greg and Vince point out, for example, after Calvin Trillin wrote about Arthur Bryant's in Kansas City, it started selling its sauce in bottles with *price codes* on them. But since the cat is out of the bag—or the pig out of the poke—let's quibble. (That's part of the fun.)

I could show off by complaining that the book doesn't mention the Wild Horse Mountain BBQ, in Sallisaw, Oklahoma: Drinks from a machine, no health certificate in evidence, a side order of jalapeños, and sauce on the ribs that seared my effete Eastern taste buds before I could tell much about the meat, but my Fort Smith friends swear by it. You'll probably get to Atlanta before Sallisaw, though, so I'll plug the Auburn Avenue Rib Shack, also un-accountably omitted. I don't know if Greg and Vince missed the Shack, or just hit it on a bad day, but it's near the Ebenezer Baptist Church and SCLC headquarters, which ought to count for something. Harold's, near the prison, gets the book's highest rating ("As good as we've ever had"); I ate there once back to back with the Rib Shack, and I'd rate it a draw.

If you get over our way, we could check out Allen and Son's, which the boys rate "Real good." Their hushpuppies went to hell about the time they put the hanging plants in, but lately they've come back strong. Or we could drive thirty miles to O.T.'s, outside Apex, which isn't in the book. O.T.'s barbecue

Famous Atlanta rib joint, closed in 1999.

Keith Allen of Allen & Son, Chapel Hill, closed in 2018.

is standard-issue Piedmont pig—that is, merely transcendentally wonderful. What keeps me and my wife going back are the accessories: great hushpuppies, and Brunswick stew that rivals the best burgoo I've ever had. O.T. is a Baptist preacher, and serves no beer, of course, but for a buck he'll give you an enormous plate of "skin"—pork rind. You can feel your arteries clog as you crunch your way through it. Research Triangle yuppies and construction workers both find O.T.'s worth the drive for lunch. Once I watched the News 5 helicopter plop down in the lot, and fly off with several plates to go.

I could go on, putting Scruggs's unrated Knoxville ribs up against Brother Jack's ("Real good"), for example. But you get the idea. If all of this means nothing to you, I'm sorry for you. If you enjoy it, you can subscribe to a barbecue newsletter that Greg and Vince have started. A recent issue included, among other things, the itinerary of a three-day, two-night, eleven-barbecue-and-one-fried-pie-joint tour of Kentucky. Better yet, get the book. Give it to your aerobics instructor for Christmas.

BARBECULTURE IN THE
TWENTY-FIRST CENTURY

In 2002 the Southern Foodways Alliance held a symposium in Oxford, Mississippi, on "Barbecue: Smoke, Sauce, and History," and I was asked to talk about "the sociology of barbecue." I'm not sure there is such a thing, but I did my best. (Incidentally, the barbecue scene in Atlanta has greatly improved.)

I DON'T THINK you can really understand the South if you don't under-stand barbecue—as food, process, and event. I recently saw a map of res-taurants affiliated with the National Barbecue Association. Of course, many of the best barbecue joints aren't the kind of establishments that would join or even know about something called the National Barbecue Association; nevertheless, that map shows plainly that (for the time being, at least) bar-becue is Southern. But it also pops up wherever large numbers of expatriate Southerners are found—no surprise, because that's usually who has cooked it: Southerners who took their tastes and their techniques and even their clientele with them during the Great Migration out of the South in the first half of the last century.

Like those migrants, barbecue followed well-established migration paths. In Oakland and Los Angeles and East Palo Alto you'll find pork ribs, to be sure, but also beef brisket and hot links and baloney—naturally, since most Southerners on the West Coast came from Texas and Oklahoma. Mississippi-ans and West Tennesseans who went to Chicago and Detroit took Memphis-style barbecue along. And in the Northeast you'll find the distinctive barbe-cues of the Carolinas and Georgia, cooked and seasoned with techniques that

James Lemons, Mississippi-born founder of Lem's, Chicago.

came north on the Chickenbone Special. One of my favorite northeastern joints, mostly because of its location, was the late Jake and Earl's Dixie BBQ in Cambridge, Massachusetts, run by Chris Schlesinger from Norfolk. To be sure, barbecue, like jazz, has sometimes changed when it left the South, and, in my opinion, like jazz, not always for the better. A few years ago I read about a New York restaurant called "Carolina," that served mesquite-grilled pork on a bed of lettuce with Dijon mustard. And my wife and I used to eat at the Arkansas Barbecue in East London's old Spitalfields Market which cooked pretty good pulled pork and brisket, but catered to British taste by serving them with mushy peas.

Anyway, barbecue may someday lose its Southern accent and become an all-American institution, as Coca-Cola did a century ago, and as NASCAR and country music and the Southern Baptist Convention may be doing today. But it hasn't happened yet. Even in the East End of London barbecue still retains its identification with the South. Which makes it odd that some conspicuous parts of the South are not especially good places to find it. South Louisiana, of course, but that's not what I'm talking about. I mean towns and cities that have got above their raisin'—or, anyway, want to get above it. Clyde Egerton has written a country song that goes "I'm a Quiche Lady in

Harold's, Atlanta (near the prison), now closed.

a Barbecue Town." Well, in some Southern towns there are a lot of quiche ladies of both sexes, domestic and imported, so many in some places that they call the shots. What you get then is a quiche town.

Atlanta is one of them. You can still find good barbecue in Atlanta, but most of the joints are hidden away off the beaten track, in obscure and sometimes unsavory neighborhoods, and some of the best have closed. It's almost as if downtown Atlanta is ashamed of barbecue—finds it too country, too low-rent.

Actually, I was being polite when I said "almost as if they're ashamed." Damn it, they *are* ashamed. When the Olympics came to town, a friend of mine from North Carolina was put in charge of arranging to feed the crowds. He lined up a local African American concessionaire to welcome the world to Georgia with a wonderful array of Southern food—most definitely including barbecue. But the Atlanta Olympic Organizing Committee was desperately eager that visitors understand that Atlanta is a cosmopolitan place (a "world-class, major-league city," as a welcome sign at the airport once proclaimed), so when the committee saw the proposed menu, they vetoed it, and hired a food-service firm from Buffalo to sell hot dogs and hamburgers.

It seems that the most quoted sentence I've ever written (you can learn

Proudly cooking Texas barbecue in Houston.

these things from Google) is, "Every time I look at Atlanta, I see what a quarter of a million Confederate soldiers died to prevent."

One of the reasons I like Texans is their attitude toward barbecue. Go to Dallas: There's Sonny Bryant's smack downtown, not far from Neiman-Marcus. Go to Houston: Goode Company's right out in public where people can find it. These places say: Welcome to Texas. Have some Texas food. We like it and you will, too.

Yes, there are Southern cities with barbecue pride. But the real home of real barbecue is in the small-town South. Not Charlotte, North Carolina, say, but Shelby, an hour west, where my wife and I go for supper when we're in Charlotte: barbecue as good as we've ever had, at Bridge's Barbecue Lodge.

Seriously, start listing great barbecue towns: The only barbecue mecca over one hundred thousand population—the only one over fifty thousand—is Memphis. (I will not speak here of Kansas City, where in fact you can get some pretty good smoked meat cooked by expatriate Southerners and their descendants. I will not speak of it because it is a Johnny-come-lately that presumes to call itself "the Barbecue Capital of the World," and it should be punished for that effrontery.)

No, the real barbecue capitals—and there's more than one—the real barbecue capitals of the world are small towns like Goldsboro, North Carolina;

Branch of a Texas barbecue chain (headquarters in Dallas).

or Lexington, where Vince Staten found sixteen barbecue restaurants for sixteen thousand people. They're places like Lockhart or Luling or Llano, Texas. They're towns like Owensboro, Kentucky (it's a distressing fact that there are now only three barbecue restaurants in Owensboro; there were eleven in 1960). The South's big cities may have barbecue, sometimes good barbecue, but it's not a religion. And, in many of them, the best on offer these days is at branches of barbecue chains. Let me say a word about that development.

I don't approve of chain restaurants in general, and I dislike barbecue chains more than most. Expansion is not good for barbecue joints. That's a rule almost as reliable as Vince Staten's maxim that a place without flies is no good. (You should ask what the flies know that you don't.) I'm sorry, but Dreamland in Birmingham just isn't as good as Dreamland in Tuscaloosa. If the owner's not around to keep an eye on things, it's a pretty safe bet that both the food and the, shall we say, *ambience* will suffer. And it's especially sad when a chain imports somebody else's traditions to a place that ought to celebrate its own. I think about this every time I eat Memphis dry ribs at Red Hot & Blue in Raleigh or Texas brisket at Dickey's in Chapel Hill. (Which is actually pretty often, because when it comes to barbecue it's almost true that the worst I ever had was good, as Dave Gardner once observed on another subject. At least I think he was talking about another subject. Sometimes it's hard to tell with Brother Dave.)

Charlotte branch of a Memphis-style chain.

Nevertheless, places with local barbecue traditions should shun synthetic tradition, or at least label it as an alien import, even if it comes from Memphis and tastes pretty good. When I have a choice I prefer the local product, ideally served up in a cinder block building with a dancing pig sign out front.

One reason I prefer it has nothing to do with the food. Go into one of these places in or near a small Southern town and you're quite likely to find that it has brought all sorts of unlikely people together, just about everyone except quiche ladies—working class and middle class, black and white and everything in-between and sideways, Protestants and Catholics, even Jews (see pp. 117–22). I once suggested half-seriously that if the South needs a new flag—as it surely does—we could do worse than to use a dancing pig with a knife and fork. You want to talk about heritage, not hate? That represents a heritage we all share and can take pride in. Barbecue symbolizes community and contributes to it. And that's without mentioning its noncommercial manifestations in matters like fundraising for volunteer fire departments, or political rallies.

I'll close by pointing out that there's another side to this coin. It's often the case—and it is in this one, too—that community is reinforced by emphasizing differences from outsiders. There's no denying that barbecue can be divisive. The only constant is slow-cooking with smoke (and, yes, I know some places cook with gas only and call their product "barbecue," but I don't). Suppose we ignore Texas beef and Owensboro mutton and go with the pork favored by the Southeastern majority. Do we cook shoulder, ribs, or whole hog? What kind of sauce—mostly vinegar? tomato? mustard? How hot? How sweet? Will we baste or not? Or forget the sauce and go with a dry rub? OK. The meat is done. What are the divinely ordained side dishes? Carolina hushpuppies? Alabama white bread? Arkansas tamales? (Check out McClard's in Hot Springs.) Coleslaw is almost universal, but I've only seen boiled white potatoes in eastern North Carolina; rice only in South Carolina; jalapeños only in Texas and Oklahoma.

These questions of what to cook, how to cook it, and what to serve with it are not resolved by the individual whim or creativity of the cook. Old-school barbecue cooks differ in technique and in skill, but they are working in traditions that pretty much tell them what to produce. And those traditions, different in different communities, reflect and reinforce the fierce localism that has always been a Southern characteristic, related to the "sense of place" that literary folk claim to find in Southern fiction. This delightful variety has come under challenge, but it is still usually possible to guess where you are from what barbecue you're served.

I hope for my grandchildren's sake that it stays that way.

WHAT CAN DWIGHT MACDONALD
TELL US ABOUT BARBECUE?

When the literary editor of *The American Conservative* asked if I would
write something for that magazine, this essay may not be what he
had in mind, but it's what he got. If affection for old institutions is
conservative, it was appropriate.

I'm pretty sure this is the first time the editor of *Partisan Review*
and barbecue have been mentioned in the same sentence.

From the colonial era well into the twentieth century, large public barbecues
were an institution across the South, from the Chesapeake eventually to
Texas. Although these occasions could be linked to campaigns or celebra-
tions of one kind or another, they could also be just an excuse for people to
get together, to eat and perhaps to drink, dance, and gamble, as well. (George
Washington won eight shillings playing cards at an Alexandria barbecue in
1769.) Often whole communities turned out. A Spanish visitor to a 1783 barbecue in New Bern, North Carolina, was amazed to see that "the leading officials
and citizens of the region promiscuously ate and drank with the meanest
and lowest kind of people, holding hands and drinking from the same cup."

Although big public barbecues can still be found, twentieth-century refrigeration and automobiles made it possible to have restaurants that serve
barbecue every day, not just on special occasions, and today that's where
most barbecue is eaten.

Fifty or sixty years ago it was easy to describe a typical barbecue place. At
its simplest it was a workingmen's "joint" that probably sold beer; at its fanci-
est it was the kind of place that attracts the after-church crowd; but often it

Community barbecue in Georgia. Photograph from *The Strand*, 1898.

Bozo's Bar-B-Q, Mason, Tennessee, in the 1950s.

was simply the community barbecue brought indoors, feeding customers of all sorts and conditions. Before the 1960s, of course, restaurants seated either black or white customers, not both, but many sold takeout for customers of the other race. In fact, some sold takeout only, but most had at least a few tables, perhaps as many as a score, and many had curb service. A place on a highway might have had drop-in business from passersby, but it was not a "destination": it served the small town or city neighborhood in which it was located. Often it was owned and operated by someone whose name was on its sign and who was usually found on the premises. If it had waitresses (or, rarely, waiters), they tended to be characters. The barbecue was cooked with heat and smoke from wood or coals.

Until the 1960s or so, most barbecue restaurants fit that description, but since then things have become more complicated.

It's easier to generalize about midcentury barbecue restaurants than about midcentury barbecue. Different communities had different traditions—whole hog in eastern North Carolina, mustard sauce in parts of South Carolina, mutton in Owensboro, "dry ribs" in Memphis, beef brisket in Texas, and so forth. Some of those traditions are actually of surprisingly recent origin, but they dictated what meats to cook and how to cook them. As Sam Jones of the Skylight Inn in Ayden, North Carolina, once put it: "When you come here it's not *what* you want, it's how much of it." Barbecue traditions even became markers of local identity, as the endless controversy between Piedmont North Carolina (tomato) and eastern North Carolina (no tomato) illustrates. The Texas-Carolina beef-versus-pork war is another example.

This vernacular form of barbecue we can call *folk barbecue*. Like other aspects of folk culture, it is tied to particular places; slow to change; inherited by communities, not created by individuals. Barbecue cooks have been esteemed for their skill, not their originality. As Deano Allen of Deano's Barbecue in Mocksville, North Carolina, once said, "People ask me why I do things this way and I say it's because everybody else always did it."

Lately, however, these traditions and the related constraints have begun to give way. To control temperatures, reduce fuel and labor costs, and placate insurance companies, for instance, many places—*most* places in the Carolinas—now cook with no wood whatsoever, not even chips to produce a little smoke, which raises the question of whether their product is barbecue at all. (The Campaign for Real Barbecue calls it "faux 'cue," but there is no applicable truth-in-packaging law.)

Another change reflects changing demand. In many parts of the South, migration has brought people from places with different ideas (or none) about what barbecue *is*. In response, many whole hog or pork shoulder places in the Carolinas have added ribs and even beef brisket to their menus; in Texas, places that proudly served their meat without sauce have begun to offer it as an option, on the side; and so forth. The customer may not always be right but even if he's wrong, he's a customer.

In an article in *Garden & Gun*, Kathleen Purvis suggested that the folk barbecue place may be an endangered species. Lamenting the closing of many North Carolina landmarks dating from the 1960s and before (most recently Chapel Hill's Allen & Son and Wilber's in Goldsboro), she observed, "It's tough to make a living off a $4 chopped-pork sandwich, especially if you have to chop down a tree to cook it." For the time being, though, despite these closures, inroads, and fallings from grace, plenty of old-time places can still be found. Hundreds of barbecue cooks across the South still labor long and hard to serve the barbecue of their people, at a price that all can afford. But theirs is no longer the only game in barbecue town.

In 2013 Josh Ozersky wrote an article in the *Wall Street Journal* about what he called "the new barbecue." About the same time, people began to refer to "elevated barbecue" (see the next chapter). *Texas Monthly*'s Daniel Vaughn

Dwight Macdonald, critic of mass culture.

wrote about a budding "big city barbecue." Others began referring to something called "artisanal barbecue" or "craft barbecue." Clearly something was emerging that needed a name.

I'm going to call it *haute barbecue*. In a 1953 essay in *Diogenes* the journalist and critic Dwight Macdonald wrote about folk culture, high culture, and popular culture. I suggest that there are now corresponding sorts of barbecue, and "haute barbecue" sounds marginally less silly than "high barbecue." (It also allows easy puns like "haute 'cue-sine" and "haute links.")

Haute barbecue differs from folk barbecue in the same ways that high culture differs from folk culture generally. While folk barbecue is passed on by tradition and tied to locality, the haute variety is produced by individual chefs (that word is used without irony) who feel free to put their own stamp on what they cook.

High culture is also produced for elite audiences, usually urban and often international. Just so, Purvis observes, "Instead of small towns and country

Cooking whole-hog barbecue in Asheville, North Carolina.

crossroads, the new barbecue temples are in cities, where they can draw more customers, both locals and visitors, who don't blanch at a $10 sandwich and a $16 mixed-meat plate."

"They charge more for food that's worth more," she writes, because these are "artisan places . . . pursuing barbecue with the intensity of a religion" and with great attention to details of ingredients and technique. Meat is likely to be "locally-sourced" and "pasture-raised," cooked with wood or wood coals (no "faux 'cue" here). Beyond that, however, haute barbecue can take different forms. Tradition may be only a starting point, if that.

Some haute barbecue chefs are neo-traditionalists, fundamentalists who cook locally traditional meats in traditional ways, but aim to do it perfectly. Austin's Aaron Franklin, who won a James Beard award for his brisket in 2015, epitomizes the type. Side dishes and desserts may be innovative, as they are at Southern Smoke in Garland, North Carolina, and The Beast, in

Tex-Mex fusion barbecue in Austin.

Paris (the French one), but the barbecue itself scrupulously adheres to tradition. Thomas Abramowicz at The Beast says, "I think the sides can be and deserve to be adapted a little to suit the French palate," but, he says, "I won't compromise on the meat." His barbecue is the genuine Central Texas stuff he learned to cook by apprenticing himself to a pitmaster in Taylor.

As Abramowicz demonstrates, one can be a neo-traditionalist in a place that has no tradition by simply importing a tradition from somewhere else. Others do the same: Buxton Hall in Asheville, North Carolina, for instance, cooks whole hogs, eastern North Carolina style, although it is more than two hundred miles west of Raleigh. Chef Michael Symon takes a different approach: his hometown of Cleveland, Ohio, has no barbecue tradition either, but he has set out to give it one. At Mabel's BBQ, Symon now serves "Cleveland-style" barbecue, using a local mustard in his sauce, seasoning with eastern European spices, and cooking with local fruitwood.

Just as classical music can incorporate themes from Negro spirituals or Hungarian folk dances, haute barbecue can take local traditions and adapt them, sometimes by blending them with other traditions. Latin or Asian influences are most common here. In Austin, for instance, Valentina's Tex Mex

PICNIC
durham

WHOLE HOG BARBECUE

Raised just up the road on Green Button Farm by Ryan Butler & his crew;
Wood-Smoked & Hand-Pulled every time by Barbecue Man, Wyatt Dickson, & his team

PULLED PORK PLATE...16.15
6 oz of barbecue served with slaw, hush puppies, and two sides

THE BOAT...9.95
just the basics ... 4.5 oz of barbecue with hush puppies and slaw

NON-NATIVE BARBECUE

SLICED BRISKET..16.50
spice-rubbed, smoked, and served with our house brisket sauce

SMOKED SPARE RIBS...18.95/28.5
spice-rubbed, smoked, & served with Aunt Perry's Rib Sauce; half or full rack

Labeling alien barbecue on the menu at Picnic,
Durham, North Carolina.

BBQ offers a classic Central Texas chopped brisket sandwich with pickles and onions alongside a smoked brisket taco with "sea salt lime guacamole and tomato serrano salsa." In Atlanta, Heirloom Market BBQ honors the Korean heritage of one of its owners by offering ribs and pulled pork marinated in *gochujang* and cooked in a Texas smoker, served with kimchi slaw and collard greens in miso. (Incidentally, these two establishments illustrate the point that haute barbecue does not necessarily mean high prices or a "fine dining" setting.)

All of these places stand in some relation to various folk barbecue traditions, but what's being announced by a Florida newspaper in an article headlined "New chef-inspired barbecue restaurant opens" is a different matter. Here we are in the presence of barbecue Protestantism, with an emphasis not on the traditional liturgy but on the barbecue equivalent of sermon and extemporaneous prayer. At these places, you're in the hands of the preacher. Floating free of any recognizable tradition, they may cook strange cuts, exotic meats, or even vegetables; put coffee or puréed blueberries in their sauces; and in general attempt to present their customers with exciting new experiences. Creativity is expected and rewarded. A British specimen I've sampled is Smokestak in London, where the signature dish is a brisket sandwich with pickled red chilies, but other examples are legion, and there are new ones every week.

Another emergent type of barbecue we can call, after Dwight Macdonald, *mass barbecue*. Like mass culture in general, it is market-driven, shaped to maximize demand, and it changes when the market changes. As I mentioned earlier, some local places are trying to cater to migrants "from away" by fixing what these newcomers want. (Picnic, a neo-traditionalist whole-hog place in Durham, has added ribs and beef brisket to its menu under the heading "Non-Native Barbecue." I think "Not from Around Here" would be better.) But we've also begun to see new places that barely acknowledge local traditions, or treat them as just one of many equally worthy options.

The logic of mass culture is that it should be the same everywhere, so it's not surprising that mass barbecue establishments are often chain restaurants, standardized and insensitive to place. Some chains are anchored in local styles, but serve it in places that have their own. Dickey's serves the barbecue of central Texas in North Carolina, for instance, while Red Hot & Blue serves Memphis barbecue in Texas. Most mass barbecue establish-

The shape of things to come?

ments, however, seek the broadest possible market by offering what I call an "International House of Barbecue" menu that mixes and matches all sorts of meats with a variety of sauces. Have it your way. The customer *is* always right. Kathleen Purvis calls the mass barbecue chains and independent restaurants that emulate them "fad barbecue restaurants," places "where you can pile Texas brisket, Memphis ribs, and Carolina chopped pork all on one plate. You can find versions in any city in the South now—look for vintage license plates on the walls and Edison bulbs dangling over the bar taps with craft brews." (Dwight Macdonald discussed the intimate relation between mass culture and kitsch.)

This "polyamorous" style (as Hanna Raskin calls it) is actually native to Kansas City, a Johnny-come-lately in the barbecue world that seems to be taking over. It is no accident that this is the sort of barbecue cooked in competitions and most often seen on television: the Kansas City Barbeque Society is the major sponsor of barbecue competitions nationwide, and its rules require that competitors, wherever they may be, cook pork butt and ribs, beef brisket and chicken. (Kansas City-style sauces are not required, but always win.)

Folk, haute, and mass barbecue are not distinguished from each other by *quality*: each can be good, mediocre, or flat bad. Nor is it a matter of *technique*: many folk barbecue places in the Carolinas now cook entirely with gas or electricity; many haute barbecue places cook with wood; the rest and

The Westland, Michigan, branch of a Minnesota barbecue chain.

most mass barbecue places at least use hybrid cookers with wood chips to produce smoke. The differences are in how each form relates to local barbecue traditions. To summarize: *Folk barbecue* is tradition-driven, geographically specific, and diverse. Different locales have different menus, each with few choices. *Haute barbecue* is chef-driven, reflecting the tastes and interests of individual cooks. Some choose to adhere to local traditions and (as they see it) perfect them; others express themselves with innovative departures from tradition. Different establishments have different menus, perhaps changing often. *Mass barbecue* is market-driven, seeking the broadest possible appeal and geographical uniformity. Ideally, in this model, there will be one menu with many choices, the same everywhere.

Haute barbecue can exist comfortably side by side with folk and mass barbecue because it is not competing for the same clientele. Patrons of haute barbecue are for the most part people who wouldn't otherwise eat barbecue. But the relation between folk and mass barbecue is more troubling.

A parable: In England, the homely native red squirrel is being driven out by the aggressive and invasive North American gray variety. Peter Coates writes that grays are the Red Delicious apples of the squirrel world; red squirrels are like endangered old-time local varieties with "peculiar names like Polly Whitehair and Bloody Ploughman." What's true of apples and squirrels is also true of barbecue. An ecologist would say that we're seeing decreasing biodiversity, increasingly uniform ecosystems. Mass barbecue is the invasive species, and its progress seems to be relentless.

I have a problem with that. For one thing, if the climax stage of the barbecue landscape leaves no room for folk barbecue it will mean the end of the community barbecue tradition. Purveyors of mass barbecue may claim that they offer something for everyone, but it's not really for *everyone*. Lawyers and construction workers, cops and college students, cowboys and hippies, preachers and sinners, rich and poor, black and white—all kinds of people used to gather in folk barbecue places like Stamey's in Greensboro, North Carolina, to eat four-dollar barbecue sandwiches for lunch, but at the International House of Barbecue the prices are higher and the "ambience" is thoroughly middle-class. (The old tools and patent medicine signs on the walls probably came from a decorator.) A guy with his name stitched over his pocket would be out of place.

Moreover, the triumph of mass barbecue will mean that you can't tell where you are by what you're eating, and that will be a shame. Peter Coates writes that concern for the red squirrel "entails the same commitment to the survival of local heritage, community identity and the ethos of diversity that invests the championing of local cheeses and apples against the tasteless universalism of international agribusiness." Well, some of us feel that way about local barbecue traditions. I've lived in North Carolina for sixty years, but I love Texas barbecue—in Texas. I love Memphis barbecue in Memphis, Kansas City barbecue in Kansas City, and even mustard-sauced South Carolina barbecue, in South Carolina. Barbecue helps to put the *there* there. Places that try to serve barbecue from everywhere are really serving barbecue from nowhere, for people from nowhere, and I say to hell with it.

YOU CALL IT ELEVATED,
I CALL IT HINCTY

The previous essay talks about how, during the twenty-teens, barbecue began to get, shall we say, aspirational. The process has gathered
momentum and seems to be irreversible, so we probably need a label
for the new stuff. In the last chapter I called it "haute" barbecue, but
that's too academic and hoity-toity for general use. "Elevated" is the
adjective that has caught on, but here's why that's obnoxious.

IN SEPTEMBER 2013 Charlotte's Bechtler Museum of Modern Art announced that a concert would be followed by a reception featuring "elevated
barbecue." That's the first example of that adjective's use I've found. It was
unusual, but you could kind of figure out what it meant. The next year a
benefit in Florence, Alabama, for the Fatback Collective Fund promised
"an exclusive, elevated barbecue experience," a new Kansas City restaurant
offered "a uniquely elevated barbecue experience in a rustic-chic environs
[*sic*]," and a place in La Brea, California, advertised a "rustic, wood-accented"
spot where diners could enjoy a "relaxed outdoor patio while savoring elevated barbecue."

Soon the phrase was everywhere—on menus, in advertising, in restaurant reviews and food writing. Although it was sometimes found in affluent,
urban Southern settings (an eighty-five-dollar VIP ticket to a Fourth of July
event in Atlanta, for instance, got you expedited check-in, roof access, and
an "elevated barbecue dinner"), it really took off *outside* the South. Within
two or three years, something called elevated barbecue was available in Philadelphia and Kittery, Maine; in Columbus, Ohio, and St. Louis, in Chicago,

Moody's Bar-B-Q in Woodbine, Georgia (not elevated).

London, a resort in the Maldives, and wherever the Norwegian Bliss cruise ship happened to be. A West Hartford restaurant "serve[d] elevated barbecue to a young, hip crowd"; one in Washington, DC, boasted "an urban garden and elevated barbecue dishes"; and the San Francisco Ritz-Carlton invited guests to "indulge in elevated barbecue-themed specials in its posh city-view Lounge."

Observe that one way to raise barbecue from its lowly roots was to serve it more elegantly or in more elegant surroundings. As a review of a new place in Houston put it: "No grinning pigs eating each other or themselves. No faux-Southern signage. No groan-inducing puns. Just a cool rectangular space with smooth wooden banquettes . . . and warmly glowing orange walls." Another new place, just down the road in Webster, was "serving elevated barbecue . . . in a table-service setting," because the owner believed that "when serving Prime Brisket, you can't serve it on trays." (On the other hand, a San Jose restaurant reviewer felt that trays were all right if used ironically; those used to serve the "impeccable, elevated barbecue fare" at a place she visited made for "an irreverent, casual and sturdy presentation completely in keeping with the culinary genre.")

A few places seem to have thought that barbecue could be elevated by décor or presentation alone, since their menus showed nothing out of the ordinary, but usually the phrase was attached to changes in what was being served. Sometimes the change was as simple as using high-quality ingredients: one Texas place, for example, was said to be "serving elevated barbecue—brisket from Creekstone Farms and USDA Prime ribeye." Sometimes the focus was on side dishes, as at an event in the Napa Valley where chefs from the Culinary Institute of America offered "an amazing menu of elevated barbecue favorites," which meant roast suckling pig served with things like roast beets, local goat cheese, salmon with burnt orange barbecue sauce, and braised collards with pickled shallots. Sometimes it was about sauces, often imported from competition barbecue: a California restaurant served sauces "made famous by Chef Charlie while competing along the BBQ circuit," and at a Kansas City place a competition veteran of fifteen years was serving sauces that included a chipotle-cilantro number to go with barbecue described as "competition quality" and "chef-driven."

"Chef" is not a word historically associated with barbecue, but chefs were all over this new development. Beer pairing dinners at a place in Lewes, Delaware, gave "the chefs the opportunity to share their elevated barbecue concepts." The motto of a St. Louis chain was "chef-inspired fine-casual barbecue." ("It's elevated barbecue," said the owner of one branch. "They take it to another level, with creative ways of doing barbecue and sides.") For some reason, Charleston, South Carolina, seems to have been a center for this sort of thing. Food writers said that one place there offered "a chef-driven menu of elevated barbecue and comfort food," another served "chef-driven, elevated barbecue," and the chef at a third "has truly taken barbecue to the next level and the elevated experience is one you don't want to miss."

Whether cooked by classically trained chefs or competition barbecuers, elevated barbecue was clearly no respecter of regional traditions: elevated Kansas City barbecue was being served in Dallas and elevated Texas barbecue in Charleston. An "American Gastro Que Pub" in Hudson, New York, served a pan-Southern menu that was not just or even primarily barbecue, but included "North Carolina pulled pork," Texas brisket, and St. Louis-style ribs. In the "rustic industrial ambiance" of Dr. BBQ in St. Petersburg, television celebrity and cookbook writer Ray Lampe was serving "nondenominational barbecue," rightly observing that Florida has no barbecue style of its own.

A frequent element was some sort of international influence. The "dining experience" at a Sacramento restaurant, for instance, "highlight[ed] elevated

Dr. BBQ, Saint Petersburg, Florida, with photo of Ray Lampe.

barbecue, in-house slow roasted meats" (basically Central Texas barbecue) with Asian touches. The menu of a new place in Wesley Chapel, Florida, incorporated Spanish and Brazilian elements, and the owner observed that "the barbecue space has been lagging behind other concepts when it comes to adopting global flavors and spices," adding that "such an elevated experience is already making its way across the country." And then there was International Smoke, a chain of "globally inspired, woodfire-infused elevated barbecue eater[ies]," where "items like smoked burrata, Korean short ribs, roasted cauliflower and St. Louis Style pork ribs" reflected cookbook writer and television personality Ayesha Curry's "Jamaican-Chinese-Polish-African-American heritage."

At some places the "elevated barbecue" was not so much innovative as just odd. In Prairie Village, Kansas, for instance, it included "classic brisket served with Cheddar cheese on grilled Texas toast," and an elevated barbecue menu in Chicago included a "Mac Daddy" sandwich with macaroni and cheese and pulled pork; and a "'Bar-B-Que Sundae' with smoked meat layered in baked beans, coleslaw, and a pickle." Others apparently used the phrase just because it sounded classy. Maybe we can give a pass to a backyard wedding in Boulder where "the idea behind [the couple's] dinner menu was elevated barbecue, so they served blackened red trout with sweet corn and roasted red pepper relish and sirloin steak served with blackberry chimichurri." After all, the steak was probably grilled. But what excuse is there for the Italian restaurant in Nashville where "dinner entrees include elevated barbecue dishes, such as braised short ribs with garlic mashed potatoes"?

But exciting new things really were happening in the barbecue world and some innovators really did deserve acclaim. Some served great, imaginative

The Granary, San Antonio.

barbecue called "elevated" by food writers who apparently just couldn't think of a more useful word. When a New York restaurant opened serving dishes like brisket ravioli and barbecued duck lasagna, for instance, the *New York Times* announced "Pig Bleecker Plans to Elevate Barbecue in Greenwich Village." Smoke, in West Dallas, which Zagat described as "chef Tim Byres' elevated barbecue joint," served cabrito, as well as flavors from Central America, the Caribbean, and West Africa. And a San Antonio guide told readers, "For some elevated barbecue in a chic atmosphere, check out the Granary," which fleshed out its Central Texas offerings with dishes like "lamb shoulder with sweet pea pudding and smoked garlic, . . . brisket ramen with smoked shoya broth and collard greens, barbecued sweetbreads with lamb, kimchi, Asian pear and lemon grass and . . . spring salad with smoked trout."

As it happens, Pig Bleeker, Smoke, and the Granary have all closed, but equally innovative places seem to be opening almost every day, and we do need a label for the kind of barbecue they cook. Personally though, I think the phrase "elevated barbecue" shows disrespect for the old-time barbecue places of the rural and small-town South. (Daniel Vaughn of *Texas Monthly* made the same point about the term "craft barbecue.") It also serves a cultural purpose that I find distasteful.

In *Pie Fidelity*, a splendid book about English food, Pete Brown writes about fish and chips, complaining that restaurants "are always trying to 're-invent' it or do it 'with a twist,' strategies which safely remove fish and chips from its [working-class] roots and allow middle-class diners to enjoy some British tradition in the safe knowledge that the working-class people who once relied upon it will not be able to afford this version." He adds, "It's not necessarily the experimentation I object to, it's the assumption that there was something wrong with the basic dish in the first place."

It's the same with barbecue. A story: In the early 1980s Gary Ford, the travel editor for *Southern Living* magazine, surveyed the South's many barbecue traditions in an article called "The South Burns for Barbecue." I'm told that Emory Cunningham, the magazine's publisher, felt that Ford's article didn't fit the genteel brand he had established, and finally published it only with deep misgivings. Cunningham was not the only country-club Southerner who associated barbecue with "joints" catering to—well, the wrong sort of people. And if some white *Southerners* thought of barbecue as Negro or redneck food, imagine what other Americans thought. I believe it's no accident that "elevated barbecue" was initially a label used most commonly outside the South. Whatever else it meant, calling barbecue "elevated" was a way to sell it to people who thought of *themselves* as elevated—that is, not working-

Smokestak, London.

class Southerners. One thing being elevated was almost certainly the price, but apparently some diners would pay to eat barbecue without fear of being defiled.

This kind of discomfort seems to follow barbecue wherever it goes. Reviewing Smokestak, a new place in London's trendy Shoreditch where a whole brisket costs £150, Grace Dent applauded the waiters' "neatly tailored all-black uniforms, resembling Madonna's Blonde Ambition dancers" and a decor that is "purposefully mature, albeit industrial, in browns, coppers, and pseudo-rusts, with dimmed lighting." The menu offered "heaven-bound sweet buns filled with impossibly good brisket littered with pickled red peppers," "crispy pig jowl on toasted challah with an alluring lavender kick," and "nuggets of pig tail as a side." This is not the stuff of "men, fire and food trucks," not "Dude food." This is "stylish wood-smoking with good, on-point service," she said. "It's grown-up barbecue. In fact, let's chuck out the B-word."

Not calling it barbecue is a radical solution to barbecue's low-rent associations even more offensive than calling it "elevated." Thank God it's a nonstarter.

But if we're still going to call it barbecue and we're not going to call it elevated, what can we call it? I called it "hincty" in my title (couldn't resist), but, like elevated, that's too judgmental. We need an adjective that is simply descriptive. Josh Ozersky called it simply "new barbecue." Daniel Vaughn has suggested "big city barbecue," because that's where nearly all of it is cooked. Jim Auchmutey, author of *Smokelore: A Short History of Barbecue in America*, suggests "gentrified barbecue." (He says that, like gentrification, "It has to do with class and polite snootiness. And it's gonna cost you more.")

Those are some possibilities, but considering that it's usually found outside the South or in Southern cities with large numbers of non-Southern migrants, I have another idea.

Why don't we call it "Yankee barbecue"?

SHALL WE GATHER
BY THE RIVER?

Some people now refer to competition barbecue as a "sport," and it's true that many competitors resemble sumo wrestlers. If it *is* a sport, it may be the fastest growing one in the country. These days hundreds of competitions attract thousands of competitors, who compete for serious prize money. Big-time winners have become television celebrities, with their own cookbooks and product lines. With so much at stake, standards for judges have become much more exacting, but when I was first a judge, in 1992, the truth is that I was judging barbecue before I knew anything about it. Damn, I had fun, though.

WHEN I WAS INVITED to be a judge at the Memphis in May World Championship Barbecue Cooking Contest some envious backbiters put it about that it wasn't because I'm well known as a discriminating *ami de swine*, but because my sister knows the woman who picks the judges. I have just one thing to say to them: Eat your hearts out.

Naturally I jumped on the chance like a dog on a—well, on a rib bone. The annual Memphis contest offers not just some of the best barbecue in the world but a complete barbecultural experience. I heard that the 1991 festival, for instance, drew entire platoons of Elvis impersonators, not to mention a contestant billing himself as "MC Hamhock" who promoted his product with a rap jingle:

Don't need no knife, don't need no fork,
Just wrap your lips around my pork.

So it was that I found myself winging over to Memphis one lovely Friday in May, eating American Airlines' peanuts and reading their copy of *Entertainment Weekly*, where I found a record review that began: "For many music fans north of the Mason-Dixon Line, contemporary white Southern culture is nothing but an *Easy Rider* cliché of booze, bikes, and bad attitude." Yeeee-haw! Pig—sooey!

On the ground in Memphis, my sister and I walked down Beale Street toward the riverside park where the contest was being held, past the usual street vendors offering assorted Afro-schlock and Deadhead tie-dye. When we came to one selling plastic pig snouts we knew we were getting close. Soon the unmistakable smell of hickory smoke assailed us and we rounded a bend into the park to behold one hundred and eighty-odd tents, booths, pavilions, kiosks, huts, gazebos, and God knows what all else stretched out before us, literally on the riverbank, just a few feet from the mighty Mississippi. It was an amazing sight, its surreality heightened by daredevil youths bungee-jumping from a crane on the bluff above us and by the tract I was given as I entered the park—a handy guide to "What to Do in Case You Miss the Rapture." (Just a tip: if you take any marks or prints on your forehead or hands you'll be sorry.)

Memphis-in-May competitors on the riverbank.

In the park we wandered about, gaping. Some mom-and-pop operations had made do with folding lawn chairs and simple funeral-home tents, but other teams had assembled two- and three-story structures with latticework, decks, statuary, and hanging plants. Each team had a name (something about barbecue seems to provoke bad puns) and many also had mottos, like "Hogs smell better barbecued." and "We serve no swine before it's time." Portable generators powered everything from electric fans to fountains to neon signs; over their drone mighty sound systems pumped out music—mostly country, Cajun, or rap, but I also caught the strains of the Village People's "YMCA."

Each team had a smoking apparatus, of course, and some had two or three. They ranged from backyard Weber pots to a tractor-trailer behemoth billed as the world's largest portable barbecue cooker, but most were roughly coffin-sized, some of them obviously off the rack, others pieced together from 55-gallon drums and stovepipe. Any doubts that barbecue contests are serious business were dispelled by the trophies on display: some teams had more brass than the US Army. And everywhere you looked you saw the pig-totem of the People of the Swine.

Now, for years I've kept a mental log of barbecue joint signs. I've seen pigs reclining, running, and dancing; pigs with bibs, with knives and forks, with crowns and scepters. I've seen pigs as beauty contest winners, pigs in Confederate uniforms, and pigs in cowboy hats (one with a banjo). I've seen Mr. and Mrs. Pig dressed for a night on the town, and Mr. and Mrs. Pig as American Gothic. But I never saw pigs like I saw in Memphis. Pigs in chefs' hats and volunteer firemen's helmets. A pig in a Memphis State football uniform triumphant over some University of Tennessee pigs. A pig in a Superman suit rising from the flames. A pig reclining in a skillet; another

Shag dancing pigs
in North Carolina.

on a grill, drinking beer. Two pigs basting a little gnomish person on a spit, and (on the T-shirts of a team called the Rowdy Southern Swine) a whole trainload of partying pigs. It's a hard call, but my favorite was probably some pigs with wings and haloes, from a team called Hog Heaven.

Italy was being honored by the festival, so a number of teams struck what they took to be Italian notes. (I gather that New Zealand, the honoree-nation the previous year, had inspired mostly tasteless sheep jokes.) Some sites were decorated with hanging bunches of plastic grapes or simulated marble columns, T-shirts said "Ciao Down," and there were almost as many Italian flags as Confederate ones. Of course the pig signs got into the act, too. Pigs ate pizza. Pigs wore handlebar mustaches. Pigs reclined in gondolas. Pigs stomped grapes. Pigs posed in gladiator gear and togas and Mafia outfits. A piece of doggerel posted in one booth combined the common themes of Italy, mortality, and beer:

> Arrivederci my pug-nosed pal
> We'll meet again at a different locale
> You in your mud, me drinking a Bud
> Way up in the final corral.

If any actual Italians were present to receive this hands-across-the-sea homage I didn't run into them, although I did meet some Swedes, who were there to see how a barbecue contest is run before starting one of their own (a scary thought). I was disappointed not to see a single Elvis impersonator. On the other hand, there were very few politicians, considering the season, and there were no street mimes at all.

In the ninety-degree Memphis heat, female attire ran to halter tops and cutoffs, often decorated with stickers saying things like "HOT," "Can't Touch This," "Roman Hands," and "USDA Choice," lovingly applied to passing butts by freelance inspectors in pig noses. I couldn't help but think of a recent, grim "feminist-vegetarian" monograph called *The Sexual Politics of Meat*. Dropped here by the banks of the Mississippi, its poor author would probably have been carried off gibbering. As a matter of fact, pig people seem to be politically incorrect on just about every score. A column in the *National Barbecue News*, for example, urged compassion for those who suffer from HIV—high intake of vegetables.

Some men wore overalls, Western clothes, or biker gear, but most wore shorts and T-shirts, often revealing all too plainly what beer and barbecue can do to the male physique. Overdressed and hot in the khakis and seersucker I'd worn on the plane, I reflected that those of us from back east have to uphold standards, but welcomed the frequent spritzes from the water guns of good-natured party animals.

At the judges' tent we encountered a man with rows of rib bones worn on his chest like decorations, dispensing stale barbecue wisdom like, "Both the pork and the cook should be well-basted." My judicial duties wouldn't begin until the next day, so we set off to take in the "showmanship" competition.

Showmanship was judged on the basis of musical routines with barbecue and Italian themes, and the strongest entries came from teams of corporation or government agency employees who brought a sort of office party atmosphere to the proceedings. "White boys can't dance," my sister muttered, as we watched one of these efforts. I reminded her that black ones probably couldn't either after drinking as much beer as some of these guys had. Shoot, they were doing pretty well to stand.

A group from South Central Bell presented a typical offering. Set in "Mama Bella's Pizzeria," it began with a grape-stomping number, followed by "Smoke Gets in Your Eyes" ("They asked me how I knew / I'd be barbecue"), a fine

The Reverend Billy C. Wirtz (author to his right, in sunglasses), on the album cover of *Backslider's Tractor Pull*.

"Barbara Ann" take-off ("You got me smokin' and a-grillin' / Sauce will be a-spillin' / Barbecue"), three girls singing "Where the Boars Are," and a mildly risqué send-up of the old Platters number, "Only You (Can Be My Barbecue)." At the end, the whole cast joined in a dance number inspired by the idea of barbecue pizza.

Inevitably, several other skits celebrated this concoction, which I gather is actually served as a regular thing at one Memphis restaurant. (I ate some at the judges' reception and it's not quite as vile as it sounds.)

Alas, the showmanship we saw was rather tame—nothing to match MC Hamhock. For genuine unglued weirdness we had to wait until that evening, when the featured act on the big stage turned out to be none other than my old Raleigh buddy the Reverend Billy C. Wirtz, down from Nashville where he moved a while back to pursue his dream. An audience of several thousand unruly Southern pork-eaters sat rapt as Billy regaled us with a song about a truck-driving lesbian from outer space and other products of his off-center mind. After the show I introduced Billy to my sister, and he took us back to his van where he gave us each a bottle of snake oil. The end to a perfect day. And the serious business of the contest—judging the pork—hadn't even begun.

Did you notice how in 1992 the national media—the *New York Times*, *Newsweek*, NPR, all of them—almost simultaneously began talking about "the Bubba vote"? I seriously doubt that many of these folks had actually met Bubba, much less discussed politics with him, but in Memphis that weekend they sure could have. Just before I went there I'd spent a couple of days in Washington, reading college professors' grant applications at the National Endowment for the Humanities. Imagine, if you can, leaving earnest consideration of such subjects as how texts reflect and resist the emergence of information as the form capital takes in the signifying environment to go hang out with the Porkaholic Beefbusters, ZZ Chop, and Pap-Paw's Pig Pokers as they deconstructed pigs, drank beer, and raised hell. I don't like to brag, but a lesser man would have suffered cultural whiplash.

Yeah, Bubba was there in force. And Tyrone was, too. (I don't think that piece of shorthand's going to catch on with NPR, do you?) Southern barbecue has always been a fine, biracial, working-class enterprise, and it still is. In Memphis, private teams were mostly all-black or all-white, but there were plenty of each, and the spectators and some corporate and government teams were unselfconsciously salt-and-pepper. We all sweltered together cheerfully in the ninety-degree heat.

But I wasn't there as a mere tourist. No, sir. I had been invited to judge the barbecue. So that evening, while the competitors were applying mysterious rubs to their meat and getting the coals just right for a long night of cooking, I headed for the Orpheum, a splendidly restored old downtown movie theater, for an orientation meeting and reception.

As I strolled up Beale Street, I reflected that there's something synthetic now, and a little sad, about Memphis's most famous boulevard. Urban renewal has turned it into a sort of Potemkin village, three or four blocks of downtown storefronts surrounded by acres of parking lots. Several clubs, including a new one owned by the great B. B. King, offer genuinely good blues, but the neighborhood's tradition has been demolished almost as thoroughly as its architecture.

From the Convention Bureau's point of view, of course, that may be just as well. The original Beale Street would have been hard to market to most out-of-towners, because its whole point was that it was a *Negro* street, the heart of black Memphis under Jim Crow. When Elvis came to Schwab's department store to buy his first sharp threads, he was making more than a fashion statement. But that time has passed and if urban renewal hadn't killed the old Beale, the end of segregation probably would have, just the way it killed black business districts in other Southern towns. Schwab's is still in business, which is something, but its window is full of tourist souvenirs.

In the absence of a living tradition, Beale Street's entrepreneurs now try to emulate New Orleans. Since my last visit, the blues clubs and obscene-T-shirt vendors had been joined by oyster bars, beignet stands, and converted Slurpee machines spewing frozen daiquiris into paper go-cups. There aren't enough drag queens yet, but my sister says they're working on it. Memphis probably needs to import some Louisiana Catholics, too: Beale Street's borderline-desperate Are-we-having-fun-yet? atmosphere feels mighty Protestant to me.

Anyway, I'd been feeling pretty smug about getting picked as a judge, but when I got to the theater I found that the honor was spread pretty thin: a couple of hundred other judges were already there. As the seats filled up, I checked out my colleagues. Some of the black folks were dressed to the nines, but shorts, T-shirts, and gimme caps seemed to be the uniform of the day for white boys. I was almost the only one in a coat and tie, the overdressed eastern dude again.

As we waited, I listened to some of my judicial brethren—guys from Kentucky and Alabama and a North Carolinian from the great barbecue town of Lexington—discuss other contests they had judged. One told me that he had completed a judge-training course offered by something called the Sanctioned Barbecue Contest Network, which sponsors some thirty major contests a year. Lord knows how many bootleg, minor-league contests there are, but the schedules in the *National Barbecue News* suggest that there are enough to keep you busy most weekends if you're inclined that way. (Later, talking to some of the contestants, I discovered that some folks are. Americans can make a way of life out of some of the damnedest things, can't we?)

Listening to these guys, I began to wonder if I was out of my depth, but I was reassured when the orientation began. Obviously I wasn't the only novice. Our instructor began with the basics ("If you don't eat pork, please let us know") and moved on to matters of deportment ("Stay sober until *after* the judging") and ethics ("If your ex-wife's boyfriend is on a team, you should disqualify yourself"). He told us that prizes had already been given for the best "area," for hog-calling, for showmanship, and for something called the "Miss Piggy in Italy" contest. (One team's Miss Piggy, I read in the paper, was provided with an honor guard of bacchae from the International Barbecue Bikini Team.) There were also prizes in a category for "other meats," which included everything from exotica like gator, snake, rabbit, and ostrich to chicken and beef (sorry about that, Texans). We were given to understand, however, that we were the elite: judges of barbecue—which starts with B, and that rhymes with P, and that stands for *pork*.

We were introduced to the rating scheme, told what to look for in the meat and sauce, and warned not to be impressed by how much money teams had spent on their areas, cookers, or uniforms. Our instructor explained why there were so many of us. There were nearly two hundred teams, he said, some with entries in more than one of the three divisions (ribs, shoulder, or whole-hog). Each entry was to be judged by six of us, and each judge was to judge only three to six entries, because you don't want your barbecue judged by someone whose taste buds have already been seared by the competition.

Fair enough. I was as ready as I was going to be.

The next morning I found the headquarters tent, checked in, and put on my special apron and judge's badge. I was to be a rib judge, and "on-site," as opposed to "blind." Each on-site judge was assigned a keeper: mine was a pleasant lady from Memphis who had done this several times before. Her job was to get me to the right places at the right times, and incidentally to rate my performance as a judge (sobriety counts, I gathered).

Waiting nervously for the tasting to begin, I talked with another judge, a man from Boston down for his seventh Memphis contest. He had taken up barbecuing to impress a girlfriend whose previous beau had been a Southerner, he said, and he assured me that he now produces the best barbecue in Massachusetts and upstate New York, which (he added modestly) ain't saying much.

At last the signal came to begin the judging. As the blind judges went into their tent, where the platters were arriving, the rest of us were led off to begin our tasting. All the fun and games, Miss Piggy and all the rest, were irrelevant now. We were down where the pork meets the palate.

I'll cut this short: the worst I had was good, but the best—cooked by a team called the Rowdy Southern Swine, from Kossuth, Mississippi—was out of this world. The smell of the smoked pork made my mouth water. When I picked up a rib and examined it, as instructed, I saw a crisp brown crust over moist

Rowdy Southern Swine and friends.

tender meat, pink from smoking, the color even from end to end. The meat came easily off the bone, but kept its integrity (none of the mushiness that comes from parboiling). This meat had been cooked with dry, cool smoke, and lots of patience. A rub sealed in the juices, but most of the fat had long since melted and dripped away. The rib tasted as good as it smelled: sweet and smoky; crunchy, chewy, and melt-in-your-mouth, all at the same time.

And the sauces . . . Well, after a quarter-century in Chapel Hill I've become fond of simple vinegar and red pepper. East Carolina minimalism. It respects the meat. But, oh my goodness, there's a lot to be said for Overmountain Baroque, too—except you can't say it without sounding like an ad in *Southern Living*: "A symphony of Southern flavors: tart Sea Island tomatoes, mellow onions from Vidalia, sweet-and-sour molasses from Louisiana cane fields, and the Latin kick of peppers from South Texas. A sauce the color of Tennessee clay, with the fiery heat of an Alabama afternoon and the long, slow sweetness of a Kentucky evening." Or, worse, like a wine critic: "A sauce of great character and finesse. Bright claret color, with a complex peppery nose. Lusty full-bodied taste: tomato ketchup and chili the principal notes, with

Taking ribs from the smoker.

a definite garlic background and hints of—could it be grape jelly? Balance sustained throughout. An assertive finish and a pronounced afterburn." I just made all that up, actually, except for the grape jelly, which I'll bet anything was the secret ingredient in one sauce I tasted. And why not? Applesauce isn't the only fruit that goes well with pork.

Anyway, I was pleased to find that I could discriminate intelligently among several first-rate plates of ribs. After I'd filled out my rating forms, I went back to two of the teams for second helpings and for the beer that I'd turned down earlier, with an eye on my keeper. I also had a pleasant chat with the Kossuth DA: small-town Southern lawyers generally know their barbecue.

I had a date for supper with my sister that evening (just a salad, thank you), so I missed the announcement of the winners, but the next morning's *Commercial Appeal* reported that the championship in the ribs division and overall Grand Championship had gone to a team from—well, from Illinois, of all places. It was no accident, either: the same guys had won two years earlier. They graciously pointed out that they come from Murphysboro, only thirty-five miles north of the Mason-Dixon line, and you have to admire them for going back to basics (no high-tech cooker, just concrete blocks with a grate and a piece of sheet metal to hold the smoke in). But, still, from *Illinois*!

It just goes to show what Yankees can do when they put their minds to it. But I'll bet the Rowdy Southern Swine had more fun.

DOWN SOUTH
IN EAST LONDON

London is tied with New Orleans as my favorite city. (I told a friend this once, and allowed as how I really didn't know what the two cities had in common. He said, "They both drink too much and drive on the wrong side of the road.") When I taught at the University of London in 2002 I was delighted to find decent barbecue at a place in Spitalfields Market. Of course it was cooked by a guy from Arkansas called "Bubba."

Since then, the market has been gentrified, Bubba has packed up his cooker and retired, and barbecue places have sprung up all over London. A few of them are pretty good.

SOUTHERNERS DON'T GO to London to eat barbecue. At least they shouldn't. But after you've been there awhile, it's understandable if you get a craving flung on you, as Jerry Clower used to say. When that happens, there's a solution.

As lunchtime approaches, take the tube to Liverpool Street Station. Go outside, cross busy Bishopsgate (be sure to look right), and turn to your left. You're on the edge of the City of London, so if it's a weekday you'll be surrounded by scurrying besuited bankers and brokers. Walk a block or so, past Artillery Lane, and turn right into Burchfield Street. (If you see the ostentatious new European Bank for Reconstruction and Development across the street on your left, you've gone too far.)

Now you're entering Spitalfields, in London's East End. Ahead is Nicholas

Hawksmoor's eighteenth-century Christ Church, recently restored to something like its original magnificence. Across the street from it is the Ten Bells pub, where Jack the Ripper met his girlfriends. In the eighteenth century this neighborhood was a haven for Huguenot refugees, who made it a center of the silk-weaving industry. Later it attracted Jewish immigrants, most of them workers and traders in fabric, leather, and furs. (They developed the Petticoat Lane street market nearby: it still operates every Sunday.) Now Spitalfields is home to the largest concentration of Bangladeshis outside Bangladesh, and if you went on past Christ Church you'd come in another block to the center of "Bangla Town," Brick Lane, famous for its great curry houses—but we're after barbecue, remember?

So turn left before you get to the church and go into the old, covered Spitalfields Market. For over three hundred years, from 1682 until 1991, this was one of London's principal fruit and vegetable markets, and there is still an organic produce market every Sunday. Parts of Spitalfields are being gentrified, as old warehouses are converted to trendy lofts, and City slickers and (rich) artists move into Georgian terrace houses that used to be sweatshops. There are plans to do over the market as well, with stuff like a tapas bar and designer boutiques, but for the time being it remains a pleasantly seedy agglomeration of stalls selling African sculptures, old phonograph records, handmade greeting cards, furniture, movie posters, clothing, and, well, schlock. Scattered here and there are vendors of fresh-squeezed fruit juice, homemade bread, Thai noodles, jacket potatoes, crepes, meat pies, goulash, falafel, nasi goreng, and other delights, but be strong: ignore them, and follow your nose.

You should get a whiff of hardwood smoke, and it will lead you to a purposely unprepossessing barbecue joint (next to the almost-as-shabby Café Mediterraneo). A large sign announces that this is the Arkansas Café. An equally large sign says, confusingly, that it is "The Bubba's [*sic*] Pit BBQ," and there are many smaller signs, among them, "We Be Ribs," "No Shoes, No Shirt, No Service," and this:

> By Appointment to His Excellency
> the American Ambassador
> Purveyors of Pulled Pork, Pigs and Ribs
> The Arkansas Café. London

This is, as one restaurant reviewer put it, "a refreshingly non-minimalist environment."

Chances are good that the proprietor, Bubba (his passport says "Kier Helberg"), will be standing outside, grilling meat and chatting with passersby.

Bubba cooks at the Arkansas Café, London.

He's *grilling*, not barbecuing: he knows the difference. Behind him stands an enormous, reassuring smoker for the barbecue, all of it cooked over split wood and charcoal. No gas cookers here, which is more than can be said for many places down home these days.

Bubba's customers include a few homesick Americans with jobs in the City, but most are simply English carnivores who come for the great steaks (including bison rib eye), brisket, sausage, country British ribs, corn-fed French chicken, and British beef and lamb burgers (Bubba says that the lambs are so attractive it's hard to get the Welsh to sell them). Most of the meat comes from the Smithfield Market, which Bubba visits every morning, but the sausages are made to his order: East Coast Polish or Italian, 100 percent pork. (He gleefully quotes someone's characterization of British sausages as "little more than disgusting abattoir waste stuffed in a Durex.") He now cooks his pulled pork only by prearrangement, for private parties or catered events. He used to have it on the menu, but didn't sell much. Most of his patrons don't deserve it anyway. One told him it looked like cat food. This from someone whose people like mushy peas.

The café also has fine side dishes, but the only ones to write home about are the yogurt-and-mint coleslaw and a scrumptious carrot cake. Bottled beer is available, at North American temperatures. The selections include some good American lagers, and British customers should be taught that there are such things, but Americans in England have no excuse for ordering Anchor Steam.

So how did an American pitmaster wind up in Spitalfields? Catch him when he's not busy and Bubba will tell you, at length.

The Helbergs were originally from Syracuse, New York, but while young Kier was growing up his father worked all over. Apparently a formative period came in El Dorado, Arkansas, when he was four or five years old. He remembers seeing a man from the Church of Christ cooking a steer with some apparatus involving chicken wire, an oil-rig pipe, and a hole in the ground. He also remembers playing cowboys and Indians with a young Billy Clinton, who was visiting relatives. The little boy from Hot Springs had a fancy cowboy outfit that Bubba coveted, and Bubba was told that was because Billy didn't have a daddy. He wondered if he'd get one if *his* daddy left.

Bubba's family soon moved on to points north and east, and eventually, after some time at the University of Maryland, he went to Johns Hopkins to study Arabic. While living in Baltimore, he patronized a barbecue and rhythm-and-blues joint called Matthew's Rib Park and another place, south of the city, called (if I've got this right) "Homer Hall's Dixie Pig Church of God Gate of Heaven also Expert Shoe Shine," where the pork was cooked on a jailhouse door laid across concrete blocks, with charcoal from barrel staves and loading pallets.

In the late '60s, newly divorced, Bubba felt the call to barbecue for himself. He bought what had been a Polish stevedores' tavern (and before that a Lumbee Indian bar and brothel called Buck's), built his own cooker, and started smoking. In 1987, he says proudly, his ribs won an award for the best in Baltimore. Meanwhile, he had begun a sideline importing antique furniture from England, and got to know Lord Rendlesham, who ran a high-toned shop in the King's Road. To make Bubba's long story short, he wound up marrying Rendlesham's daughter, the Honourable Sarah Thellusson, and moved to London. (The Hon. Sarah is also very much a presence at the Arkansas Café and, oddly enough, not at all an incongruous one. The coleslaw is her recipe.) Sometime in the late '80s Bubba and Sarah decided to throw a Fourth of July party. Bubba made a primitive smoker out of garbage cans (he has been in England long enough now to call them "dustbins") and cooked some barbecue. It was a hit, and someone asked him to do it again for a party at Lloyd's Bank. Before he knew it, Bubba had a catering business going; it did so well that he got his barbecue gear out of storage in the States, shipped it to London, and opened the Arkansas Café in 1991 in the newly vacated market. He has been there ever since, and let's hope he doesn't get pushed out when the place gets tarted up.

By the way, the sign about "appointment to the American ambassador" is no joke—or at least not entirely a joke. It dates from the tenure of Admiral William Crowe as ambassador in the mid-'90s. Crowe, an Oklahoman, engaged Bubba to cater his Fourth of July garden parties, serving up to four thousand guests at a time. It's a shame that the present ambassador, William Farish, though a Texan, apparently hasn't discovered the best brisket east of Land's End, but Bubba doesn't have any hard feelings about that: after 9/11 he cooked some free pig for the volunteers who managed the flowers and book of condolences in Grosvenor Square.

REAL BARBECUE

THE CAMPAIGN FOR
REAL BARBECUE

In the 1970s, when English pub beer, drawn directly from a cask containing live yeast, was threatened by new, processed, artificially carbonated beers, the Campaign for Real Ale was founded to champion the traditional product. Something similar has been going on with barbecue, and it's time for a Campaign for Real Barbecue.

A SPECTRE IS haunting the South—the spectre of smokeless "barbecue." Consider the case of North Carolina, where the situation is particularly grave.

Ever since early colonial days, barbecuing has meant cooking meat over hardwood coals, and in North Carolina barbecue, as a noun, eventually came to mean whole hogs or pork shoulders cooked that way. By the middle of the twentieth century, North Carolina was recognized as the center of one of the nation's major barbecue regions, and barbecue was central to the state's culinary culture, found at scores of community pig-pickings and literally hundreds of humble barbecue restaurants.

In the 1970s, however, we Tar Heels lost our way. Some blame a man named Bob Fulp, the head of the state's environmental affairs department, who began a campaign to get barbecue restaurants to change to gas or electric cookers, supposedly to improve air quality. For whatever reason—perhaps just because cooking with gas or electricity is cheaper and easier than wood-cooking—many restaurants made the switch, and by century's end the great majority of North Carolina "barbecue" places, including some of the oldest and best known, no longer used wood or charcoal at all. This is sad. Even sadder is that many customers either didn't notice or don't care. Out of stubbornness

Smokehouse at Stamey's, Greensboro, North Carolina.

or pride a few places clung to the old ways, but a restaurateur in Raleigh exaggerated only a little when he unashamedly told the Food Network that "around here we use hickory for canes."

By 2013 two of us had had enough. Dan Levine (aka "Porky LeSwine," impresario of BBQJew.com) and I (a retired professor with time on my hands) founded the Campaign for Real Barbecue. We had three aims in mind: (1) to celebrate and promote barbecue's wood-cooking heritage; (2) to educate the public about the barbecue tradition and the difference between real wood-cooked barbecue and what we call faux 'cue; and (3) to identify and honor places that still cook in the traditional way. (To be clear, we reserve the "faux

Look for the True 'Cue label.

'cue" label for meat cooked in the complete absence of smoke; we have no beef with those who use gas or electricity for ignition and temperature control.)

Our principal activity so far has been tracking down restaurants that cook the old-fashioned way, entirely with wood or charcoal, listing them on our website for the benefit of discerning eaters, and giving them certificates and decals that show they have been endorsed by the campaign. At this writing we have "certified" about seventy North Carolina establishments that qualify. (Unfortunately, since we started this list a half-dozen places have closed or switched to gas or electricity.)

We hope in time to take the campaign nation- or at least South-wide, because what has happened in North Carolina is only an advanced form of what is happening in some other places. We already have branches in South Carolina, Kentucky, Georgia, and Virginia. (Texas may not need us: I suspect that a Texan who cooked meat with gas and called it barbecue would be shot, or at least mocked. I say, good for Texas.) TrueCue.org, our website, offers lists of certified restaurants, a compendium of testimonials to the importance of wood-cooking, an essay on the slippery slope between real pit barbecue and crock pot "barbecue," a list of some forty barbecue historians, documentarians, bloggers, cookbook writers, and other "patrons" who have endorsed our efforts, and much else. Coverage of our certification program and other campaign news can be found on our Facebook page. For an outfit that's basically just a handful of volunteers, we have received a good deal of press, notably a story by Calvin Trillin in *The New Yorker*, called "In Defense of the True 'Cue."

In the words of Pete Jones, founder of the Skylight Inn in Ayden, North Carolina, "If it's not cooked with wood, it's not barbecue."

From the Raleigh, North Carolina, yellow pages, 1952.

WHAT IS REAL BARBECUE?

If you're going to campaign for real barbecue, you have to say what it is. Here's the Campaign for Real Barbecue's manifesto. Some of us Southerners are drawn to lost causes: This may be another one, but it's worth fighting for.

The answer isn't simple. There's a continuum between what is undeniably and gloriously the real thing and that which clearly is not.

At the pinnacle of the pitmaster's art is barbecue cooked the traditional way, entirely with heat and smoke from burning hardwood or hardwood coals. What meat or meats are cooked, what sauce is used (if any), the details of cooking techniques—these are given by tradition as well, but traditions vary from place to place. The one constant is wood, the source of heat and smoke.

Tennesseans, Texans, Midwesterners, and federal bureaucrats don't agree about much, but all understand that cooking with hardwood makes the difference between barbecue and roast meat. The Memphis in May World Championship Barbecue Cooking Contest and all its tributary contests define barbecue as "pork meat only . . . prepared on a wood or charcoal fire." The Kansas City Barbecue Society is more permissive about meats, but uses exactly the same language about how the cooking should be done: "on wood or charcoal fire." Contests run by the Central Texas Barbecue Association also stipulate that "under no condition can gas or electricity be used for cooking." And the Code of Federal Regulations, Title 9, Subpart CFR § 319.80, defines

Burning down to coals at Wilber's Barbecue, Goldsboro, North Carolina.

barbecue as "cooked by the direct action of heat resulting from the burning of hardwood or the hot coals therefrom."

Cooking the old-school way, entirely with wood, is still the preferred method for those like competition barbecuers who have the time and resources for it. But technology marches on. In towns and cities from sea to shining sea, barbecue is now being prepared with something like Ole Hickory or Southern Pride cookers, hybrid devices that use wood for smoke but supplement it with some degree of heat from gas or electricity. At its best this process can produce barbecue on par with the entirely wood-cooked variety, and does so more consistently with less oversight. It is also easier and cheaper, so it's no surprise that most new barbecue restaurants these days take this course, some of them with excellent results.

But the product of hybrid cookers doesn't always measure up to the gold standard of all-wood cooking. Hybrid devices can be used simply as gas or electric ovens, with a few wood chips feebly smoking—not much different from roasting meat and then giving it a pass through a stove-top smoker. The next step in this downward spiral is cooking with no wood at all. There actually are establishments, all too many of them, that serve slow-roasted meat untouched by even the bottled kind of wood smoke and call it barbecue.

You see the problem. We start with barbecue cooked in a pit over live coals, or with heat and smoke from a stick-burning firebox, and we end up with a Boston butt in a crockpot. Somewhere along the way we've crossed the line between True 'Cue and faux 'cue. We do not intend to draw that line, just to point out that there's a hierarchy here and the purveyors of faux 'cue are at the bottom of it. (We won't name and shame these folks, but they know who they are and they know what they can do about it.)

Why do we care? Because we believe that Real Barbecue is rooted in three things increasingly lacking in today's world: taste, tradition, and a sense of place. Because we think the world will be a better place with more Real Barbecue in it.

FUEL FOR THE FIRES OF HELL

The devil makes them do it. From *True 'Cue News.*

FROM
TRUE 'CUE NEWS

The Campaign for Real Barbecue's newsletter is devoted for the most part to news of the campaign's certification efforts, but from time to time it has discussed how the campaign works, reported other news from the world of barbecue, and printed True 'Cue–themed cartoons. Here are a few examples.

WOOD-COOKING ON HAIGHT STREET

Most East Coasters who hear "Haight Street" probably think of going to San Francisco and wearing flowers in their hair. A few of us, however, think of Memphis Minnie's, an unprepossessing joint that cooks some of the best barbecue west of Texas, entirely with wood. At Minnie's they don't even use gas for ignition; they start the fire with a chimney-full of charcoal briquettes.

Minnie's was the baby of Bob Kantor, a Brooklyn guy who made a real study of the Southern barbecue tradition and brought it to the Bay Area, with a few of his own West Coast touches like sake, vegan collards, and pastrami once a week. Since Bob's untimely death in 2013, Minnie's has changed hands a couple of times, but last time I was there it was still faithfully continuing Bob's legacy, sake and all.

Whenever someone tells us that they're not allowed to cook with wood, we tell them that if Minnie's can do it in downtown San Francisco, it can be done anywhere.

Memphis Minnie's, wood-cooking on Haight Street, San Francisco.

DO WE TELL RESTAURANTS
HOW TO RUN THEIR BUSINESS?

As Nathan Bedford Forrest is supposed to have said, "I done told you twice already goddammit no!" But the accusation persists. So once more: We aim simply to identify and honor places that cook old-school. You got a problem with that?

Look, there are many restaurants, especially in the Carolinas, that cook entirely with gas or electricity. We try to avoid them ("except when courtesy requires it," as the True 'Cue Pledge puts it)—and it's true that we refer to their smoke-free product as "faux 'cue," but we don't tell them how to run their business. In fact, we don't even name them. Places like Homegrown Smokehouse & Deli in Portland, Oregon, which cooks "pulled pork–style soy curls"—them we *will* name, but even them we don't tell how to run their business.

BARBECUE INSTITUTIONS

One reason the Campaign for Real Barbecue doesn't name and shame restaurants that serve mere roast pork and call it "barbecue" is that some of them are among the oldest and best-known places around and have earned some respect for their history and their role in their communities. A long-established small-town barbecue place with pictures of the high school football team on the wall, the kind of place where the after-church crowd goes, the Lions Club meets, couples court and celebrate anniversaries—a place like that deserves some tolerant silence, even if its food is mediocre, or worse.

"Sometimes it's not the best food," says Alton Brown, host of the Food Network's *Good Eats*, "but you have to look at its place in the community. It's funny with barbecue, because the most beloved barbecue places in the South, by and large, serve the shittiest barbecue."

OK, an overstatement, but he was on his way to making an important point: "Places that people will drive hours to get to, barbecue's not that great, but it's still there. It's been there. My mom brought me here. My grandparents are from here. I love this place. In the end, authenticity and a sense of place are more important than taste and flavor. That's something that we forget in our Instagram craze—that place and authenticity, history, all matter. That's what really connects us to a place. Good food isn't always the most important." We at the campaign are concerned with good food, but we wouldn't argue with that.

GOOD NEWS AND BAD FROM WINSTON-SALEM

The bad news is that some anonymous vigilante has been waging a campaign against the smoke from the pits at Little Richard's Barbecue (now renamed Real Q), complaining to the county environmental protection department

Wood smoke and kudzu at Little Richard's, Winston-Salem, North Carolina.

that "the plume . . . at Mr. Richards [*sic*] contains hickory smoke laden with grease from burned hogs and hush puppy grease." (Yum.)

The good news is that he was told essentially that the county can't do much about smoke coming from restaurants. The Clean Air Act applies only to industrial facilities and processes, the director of the department said. "We'd be guilty of governmental overreach if we tried to enforce industrial standards on restaurants."

How great to hear the phrase "governmental overreach" from a government official!

A WORD ABOUT THE CAMPAIGN'S PATRONS

At last count, forty-six worthy folk had consented to support the Campaign for Real Barbecue by lending their names as patrons. Since they represent a dizzying variety of barbecue traditions, drawn from both Carolinas, Georgia and the Deep South, Kentucky, Memphis, Texas, Kansas City, and elsewhere—some nineteen states and the District of Columbia—they don't agree about much, but they do all agree that *real* barbecue is cooked with wood smoke.

As our website says, our patrons "are primarily eaters and critics of barbecue, and students of its history and culture." Most cook barbecue at home, many have judged barbecue competitions, and a few have run restaurants,

The Secret Life of Hank Hill.

but, to our knowledge, none now competes regularly or cooks barbecue for a living. This has rankled a few people who *do* cook it for a living. One restaurateur, miffed at what he mistook to be disrespect on our part, wrote, "I can assure you that they [i.e., us, the campaigners] are not experts." He dismissed us as "writers, not pitmasters." What we see here, of course, is the age-old tension between creator and critic. Brendan Behan, speaking for the artists, asserted: "Critics are like eunuchs in a harem; they know how it's done, they've seen it done every day, but they're unable to do it themselves." Behan had a point, but we stand with Aristotle, who wrote twenty-four hundred years ago, "The diner judges a banquet better than the cook."

BROOKLYN BARBECUE

A recent Vice.com article headlined "Why Is Brooklyn Barbecue Taking Over the World?" naturally provoked a lot of outrage and trash talk. In fact, if you read the whole article, you'll find that the author, Nicholas Gill is *almost* appropriately humble, but his provocative headline (which he didn't write) couldn't pass without comment. Perhaps the best response was a *Washington*

Hometown Bar B Que, wood-cooking in Red Hook, Brooklyn.

Post article, especially the "correction": "An earlier version of this story incorrectly located Brooklyn in the Canadian province of Quebec." (The article now says that Brooklyn is "a fast-growing suburb of Poughkeepsie, N.Y.") The comments reveal that many *Washington Post* readers have no sense of humor.

We'll just observe that there has been barbecue in Brooklyn at least since the late George H. Lee started trucking it in from his native Duplin County, North Carolina, to sell in a gas station parking lot. But Bedford-Stuyvesant is being gentrified, and its barbecue is, too. What the article means by "Brooklyn barbecue" is the product of cultural appropriation by hipsters with tattoos. What they cook can be excellent—don't get us wrong—but any claim of world domination is, to say the least, premature.

BUSTING A BARBECUE MYTH

Why would someone switch from wood-cooking to gas or electricity? People have lots of excuses, but one of the ones most often heard is, to put it no more strongly, based on a misconception. One of the Campaign for Real Barbecue's missions is education, so let's start with this.

FOR OVER THREE HUNDRED YEARS barbecue in North Carolina was cooked for a long while at a low temperature over hardwood coals. Those coals were what made the difference between barbecue and roast meat. But, sadly, these days wood-cooked barbecue is getting hard to find. Many "barbecue" restaurants—*most* barbecue restaurants in North Carolina—have stopped cooking with wood, or never did. Outsiders are starting to notice, and our state's longstanding reputation for barbecue excellence has begun to suffer. Lolis Eric Elie, the author of *Smokestack Lightning*, remarked recently that "there are far more gas and electric pits [in the Carolinas] than in other parts of barbecue country," and called it "a disturbing trend that needs to be reversed." The late Bob Kantor, who cooked with wood on Haight Street in San Francisco at Memphis Minnie's, professed himself "puzzled and deeply concerned at what appears to be a trend in North Carolina towards substituting gas and electric for wood." And Jim Shahin, barbecue columnist for the *Washington Post*, has observed, "Gas has made many inroads into North Carolina barbecue and the authentic wood-only barbecue there is in some jeopardy." I could go on.

Since 2013 the Campaign for Real Barbecue has been working to identify and to applaud those barbecue places that still cook in the old-school way,

Alston Bridges Barbecue, in Shelby, North Carolina.

to encourage new "artisanal" wood-cooking barbecue establishments, and to persuade gas-cookers to return to the True Faith.

It is true that cooking with gas or electricity is cheaper and easier, and the product is more consistent (if not great). But when we ask gassers why they don't cook with wood, they seldom mention those considerations. Instead, we almost always hear stuff like, "The city won't let us," or "The inspector made us stop," or "It's against the Clean Air regulations." In short, the government made them do it.

But this never comes with specifics. No one has ever been able to tell us exactly what regulations make it impossible. In fact, the only regulations we've seen in print actually require that if meat is sold in grocery stores and labeled "barbecue," it *must* be cooked with wood. Nobody expects governments to be consistent, but why would they turn around and forbid barbecue to be wood-cooked when it's sold in restaurants? (And why would wood-fired pizza ovens get a pass?)

So, in the April 23, 2014, issue of the *Raleigh News & Observer*, we issued (fanfare, please) the True 'Cue Challenge. We offered a handsome "No Faux 'Cue" apron to the first person to identify (1) any statute or regulation that forbids any North Carolina barbecue restaurant to cook with wood or charcoal, or (2) any official—federal, state, county, or municipal—who has made a North Carolina barbecue restaurant stop cooking with wood or charcoal, or who has forbidden one to start. "If there really are laws or regulations that make life difficult for wood-cooking barbecue restaurants," we wrote, "we will work to change them. If there really are bureaucrats undermining our state's barbecue heritage, the Campaign will reason with them—and, if reason does not suffice, we will denounce and vilify them."

Several people got in touch to thank us for what we're doing, and one man wanted to argue that his gas-cooked pork is as good as the genuine article (it's not). But no one even tried to meet the challenge. When no one had claimed the prize after a year, we upped the reward to include a True 'Cue ball cap.

The challenge still stands. We are increasingly convinced that any restaurant anywhere can cook barbecue with wood if it really wants to.

TAR HEEL 'CUE

BBQ & A

★ ★ ★

From 2009 to 2015 Dan Levine ("Porky LeSwine") ran a website called BBQJew.com, devoted to North Carolina barbecue (motto: "When the Chosen People choose pork"). He interviewed my wife and me about our book on the subject.

BBQJEW: Husband and wife writing team John and Dale Reed have written an instant classic, *Holy Smoke: The Big Book of North Carolina Barbecue*. And considering that they have a Jewish son-in-law and have lived in Israel, we welcome them into the fold as honorary BBQ Jews. (We're an inclusive people.) The 'cue-loving couple were kind enough to share some swine with us and to put up with our questions.

BBQJEW: How many plates of barbecue would you estimate you have eaten?

DALE: We've each probably eaten something between five hundred and a thousand plates, starting at Turnage's in Durham in 1961 or so. That works out to—what?—only two or three hundred pounds.

JOHN: Not all that much, compared to some folks we know.

BBQJEW: John, when you taught at Hebrew University in Jerusalem, did you find any good barbecue in the Promised Land (perhaps basted with milk and honey)?

JOHN: No barbecue, although we occasionally bought pork chops from a Christian Arab butcher who mostly sold to the embassies.

Holiday card from BBQJew.com.

DALE: Very occasionally, because they were very expensive.

BBQJEW: What brought you to write *Holy Smoke*?

JOHN: We were eating barbecue one evening with David Perry, the editor-in-chief at UNC Press, and we discovered that he and I both cooked out of a book called *Legends of Texas Barbecue*, by a friend of ours named Robb Walsh. Someone at the table—we really don't remember who—said, "You know, somebody ought to do something like this for North Carolina."

DALE: John and I sort of looked at each other and said, "We will!"

JOHN: So we sent David a proposal, and the press bought it.

DALE: We knew William McKinney when he was a UNC undergraduate and the founder and moving spirit of the Carolina Barbecue Society, and we knew he'd videotaped interviews with some of the great names in North Carolina barbecue, so we got him on board as soon as we could.

JOHN: William's also our whole-hog cooker. The instructions for doing that and for building a pit are his. Me, I cook shoulders, but I'm happy to leave whole-hog cooking to the professionals.

BBQJEW: In researching the book, did you come across any fellow Jews involved in North Carolina barbecue in any way?

JOHN: Well, none of the pitmasters or restaurant owners. Actually, though, I think two of the eight guys we listed as Chevaliers du Tasty Swine—champions of the cause—are Jewish. Barry Farber's a UNC grad who has made a career as a radio talk-show host in New York and who experimented back in the '70s with a North Carolina barbecue joint in New York.

DALE: He got the real stuff flown in flash-frozen from Fuzzy's in Madison, but he gave up when he went in one day and found the Greek guys who were running the place serving the barbecue on bagels.

JOHN: Alexander Julian's the other. He's the big-time New York fashion designer from Chapel Hill who took payment in barbecue for designing the Charlotte Hornets' uniforms. He gets frozen barbecue shipped to him regularly.

Sign at Corky's, Memphis.

DALE: We know a good many Jews in other states who are in the barbe-cue business, starting with Gershon Weinberg, who used to run the Old Smokehouse Barbecue in Anniston, Alabama, and going on to our buddy Bob Kantor, a Brooklyn guy who ran Memphis Minnie's, a terrific wood-cooking place on Haight Street in San Francisco. Corky's, one of the biggest Memphis barbecue places, is owned by a Jewish family. They're best known for their pork ribs, but they have a dedicated kosher cooker to cook brisket for the Jewish community.

JOHN: You know a piece by Marcie Cohen Ferris in *Cornbread Nation 2* called "We Didn't Know from Fatback"? It's got to be the last word on the subject of Jews and barbecue.

BBQJEW: We prefer to think of it as the first word. We hope to have the next. OK, let's say Yom Kippur is ending and it's time to break the fast. BBQJews of all stripes are depending on you to recommend the restaurant that serves the most divine swine in the nation. Where do you send them?

JOHN: Look, there are a couple of dozen places in North Carolina that we wouldn't hesitate to recommend. Shoot, there are a half-dozen in Davidson County. On a given day, any one of them might have the best barbecue in the state (which means, of course, the best in the nation).

DALE: On a particular day, our advice might be terrible, because any wood-cooking place is going to have good days and bad days. You want one that doesn't have many bad days and that doesn't need a good day to cook great barbecue.

JOHN: Yeah, if you want uniformity, go to a place that cooks with gas or electricity. You'll get uniformly mediocre barbecue. At best, uniformly OK.

BBQJEW: An artful dodge. You guys are good. At gunpoint: Eastern- or Lexington-style?

JOHN: This answer's not going to make anybody happy, but whichever is nearer. You sometimes get the sense that partisans would rather have a second-rate plate of their own style than a first-rate plate of the other. Not us.

DALE: If I had to choose between excellent examples of both, I'd probably go with Piedmont-style, because I really, really like "outside brown" and you get more of it with shoulders—especially if you know to ask for it.

JOHN: She just says that because her people are German.

DALE: We make a big deal in our book about the German origins of Lexington-style.

JOHN: I'd be hard pressed to say. I would have agreed with Dale once. But the more I've learned about this, the more I like Eastern-style. In part, that's because I'm a traditionalist, and Eastern-style is pretty much what barbecue was everywhere for most of the nineteenth century. It carries the weight of all that great history. But there's more to it than that. A guy named Steve Stephens called North Carolina barbecue "the crack cocaine of pork"—he meant you can't put it down—and Lexington-style is like the gateway drug for folks who didn't grow up with it. The sauce is sweeter, as a rule, it has that tomato tang, and the meat has fewer surprises in it. It may be easier for the uneducated palate to like. But once you've come to like the vinegar-based sauces of the Piedmont, you find yourself wanting something more . . .

BBQJEW: We're petitioning the Orthodox Union to create a law pronouncing wood-cooked barbecue to be kosher. Would you back that rule change and are there any other general barbecue laws you would like to see?

DALE: We'd like to see a ruling that anything rubbed with kosher salt isn't treyf.

BBQJEW: What's the most important thing you look for in a barbecue restaurant?

JOHN: Barbecue. I'm not being facetious; the meat's what matters, at least as far as I'm concerned. I don't give a damn about the décor or the "ambience." As our buddy Vince Staten says, "My taste is mostly in my mouth."

DALE: Me, too. We also don't care (much) about the side dishes or the desserts or the wine list, or even the service. If the barbecue's mediocre, nothing else matters. If the barbecue's great, nothing else matters.

BBQJEW: Do you have a barbecue joint pet peeve?

DALE: We've become fundamentalist about wood-cooking. Good barbecue can be cooked with hardwood charcoal out of the bag, but out of the burn barrel is better. And fossil fuels should be banned.

JOHN: We don't bother with gassers, which has saved us a good deal of time and money over the years. Of course, sometimes we bend that rule for social reasons. It might be impolite to refuse an invitation, for instance, or we might just not want to offend friends by disrespecting the barbecue at their favorite restaurant. Sometimes you can get away with ordering the vegetable plate.

BBQJEW: John, we've seen a photo of you in your military uniform from your teaching days at The Citadel. Might there be a photo from Hebrew University of you sporting a yarmulke?

JOHN: Yeah, when in Rome . . . As a matter of fact, there's a photo Dale took of me and our kids at the Seder we went to in Jerusalem in 1974. I'll send it to you.

Pesach in Jerusalem (author and daughters at left).

THE PIEDMONT REFORMATION
(WITH DALE VOLBERG REED)

My late wife was a crackerjack genealogist, and this contribution to barbecue history is based on her research. Others had speculated about the German connection to Piedmont North Carolina barbecue, but she nailed it down.

In eastern North Carolina and adjoining parts of Virginia and South Carolina, barbecue is a matter of whole hogs or other animals cooked over hardwood coals and dressed with a mix of peppers, salt, and vinegar (and/or lemon juice). This procedure has been essentially unchanged since the *Richmond Enquirer* reported in 1829 that a gourmand's "favorite barbacue . . . is a fine fat pig called 'shoat,' cooked on the coals, and highly seasoned with cyane [cayenne]."

The recollections of Martha McCulloch-Williams, the daughter of a North Carolina tobacco planter who moved to Middle Tennessee, are of special interest. In *Dishes & Beverages of the Old South* (1913), she gave instructions for roasting lamb and pork in the oven, "as near an approach to a real barbecue, which is cooked over live coals in the bottom of a trench, as a civilized kitchen can supply," and shared her memories of barbecues when she was a young girl (she was born in 1848). Whole lambs, pigs, and kids were cooked on open pits, basted with salt water "and turned over once only," then served with her father's "dipney," or finishing sauce, which was simmered for half an hour, then mopped, hot, onto the cooked meat: "Daddy made it thus: Two pounds sweet lard, melted in a brass kettle, with one pound beaten, not ground, black pepper, a pint of small fiery red peppers, nubbed and stewed

Cooking whole hogs Eastern-style in Rocky Mount, North Carolina.

Cooking shoulders Piedmont-style in Lexington, North Carolina.

soft in water to barely cover, a spoonful of herbs in powder—he would never tell what they were,—and a quart and a pint of the strongest apple vinegar, with a little salt."

This sauce, or something very much like it, became the standard almost everywhere. Martha's daddy had evidently taken his Tar Heel tastes and techniques with him when he moved west (and to this day thin, vinegar-based sauces can be found in places like Lexington, Tennessee, and Blytheville, Arkansas). In 1896 *Harper's Weekly* reported an almost identical sauce from

Georgia, also called "dipney" (surely the origin of the word "dip," used for sauce in the Piedmont—and Kentucky). Lettice Bryan's *Kentucky Housewife* (1839) has one that sticks with lemon juice instead of vinegar, and a traveler outside San Antonio in 1883 found a similar sauce even in Texas, except with cow butter instead of hog lard.

Meanwhile, back in East Carolina, Sarah Frances Hicks, a Yankee married to a North Carolinian, wrote home to New York from Greene County in 1853: "Red pepper is much used to flavor meat with the famous 'barbecue' of the South & which I believe they esteem above all dishes is roasted pig dressed with red pepper & vinegar."

Other places might have strayed from this tradition, but eastern North Carolinians kept the Faith. As far as they were concerned, perfection had been pretty much attained Before the War, and their barbecue now is more or less what barbecue was then.

About the time of World War I, however, a new and competing version of barbecue emerged in the hills of the North Carolina Piedmont. When early barbecue entrepreneurs in the East started selling barbecue by the sandwich or the plate, they were working in an established tradition, purveying the same peppery-vinegary whole-hog pulled pork that people had already been eating at community and family barbecues. But the first barbecue stands in Lexington and Salisbury were cooking just parts of the hog—loins, hams, and especially shoulders. And they served their barbecue in slices, as well as chopped or pulled. In an even more radical departure from tradition, they were lacing the classic vinegar and pepper sauce with tomato ketchup.

Although these innovations had precedents in domestic cookery, they were something new in the North Carolina barbecue world, and they were viewed by many Easterners with much the same enthusiasm that the medieval Catholic Church had for the Protestant Reformation. North Carolinians have been arguing about this ever since.

But why these particular innovations?

The humble creators of the Eastern tradition are known to God alone, but the pioneers of Piedmont-style have names: John Blackwelder of Salisbury; Sid Weaver, George Ridenhour, and Jess Swicegood of Lexington; and, a little later, Warner Stamey of Lexington, Shelby, and finally Greensboro. It's said that you are what you eat, but it's equally true that you eat what you are—and in one respect these men were all the same thing:

John Blackwelder's family had been in Mecklenburg, Cabarras, and Rowan Counties since soon after Gottlieb Schwartzwalder came from Germany to British North America before the Revolution.

George Ridenhour's people came to Salisbury in 1779 from Pennsylvania, where the Reitnaurs first settled after coming from German-speaking Alsace in 1719.

Jess Swicegood's family came to America from Germany in 1724 and also passed through Pennsylvania before settling in Davidson County in 1775 and Americanizing their name from Schweissgouth.

Sid Weaver's antecedents are a little more elusive, although many North Carolina Weavers started as Webers, and his ancestor Andrew was listed as "Andras" in the 1860 census.

The North Carolina Stameys—Warner included—are all descended from a Peter Stemme who came from Germany in 1734 and made his way down the valley of Virginia to what is now Lincoln County in 1767.

Can you spot the common element? Of course you can. When you add maternal lines these family trees are as full of Germans as a Munich beer hall at Oktoberfest. Compare those family names to the big names in Eastern barbecue: good British ones like King, Parker, Jones, Ellis, Shirley, and Melton, no matter whether they're affixed to white families or black ones.

Sid Weaver and George Ridenhour at their stand in Lexington.

It's not exactly news that Piedmont North Carolina has had a substantial German presence since the "Dutch" started coming down the Great Wagon Road from Pennsylvania in the 1700s. This is still evident in the names found in telephone books and in the Lutheran and Reformed churches on the landscape. But until historian Gary Freeze (originally Friess?) at Catawba College got interested in it, their role in shaping Tar Heel cuisine—liver mush aside—had been largely neglected. (Freeze notes that the early Lexington barbecue men got their shoulders from Conrad and Hinkle—Conrath and Henckel?—old-style grocers still operating in downtown Lexington, who raised the pigs themselves.)

The German influence in North Carolina has been more subtle than that of the German butchers in Texas who made sausage and beef brisket major parts of the Lone Star story, or that of South Carolina's upcountry Germans who introduced, and sell to this day, their state's peculiar mustard-based sauce. (Lake E. High Jr. of the South Carolina Barbeque Association points out the continuing importance of families with names like Bessinger, Shealy,

Lexington grocery store at the same location since 1919.

Hite, Sweatman, Sikes, Price, Lever, Meyer, Kiser, Zeigler, and Dooley—originally Dula, as in Tom, of Wilkes County and the Kingston Trio song.) But in North Carolina the German factor is obvious once you start looking for it.

In all of German-speaking Europe pork was the meat of the peasant classes, and in the New World their descendants remained attached to it. When Germans and their hog-droving Scotch-Irish contemporaries arrived in the 1700s they fit right in to porcivorous North Carolina. To this day German cookery has a particular fondness for *smoked* pork, sometimes marinated in vinegar flavored with various spices; the Pennsylvania Dutch cousins of North Carolina Germans, for example, cook a dish called *saurer Seibrode*, basically a pork version of *Sauerbraten*. True, the smoked pork of German cuisine is salted or brined, smoked in a smokehouse, and soaked in water before being cooked, but the point is that vinegar-and-smoke-flavored pork was not an alien taste for German newcomers in North Carolina. All that was lacking were the cayenne peppers.

Here's the clincher. William Ways Weaver, who writes about the history of German and Pennsylvania Dutch cooking, points out that the shoulder of the hog was a particularly esteemed cut, indeed a "ritual consumption item" at hog-killing time, and *Schäufele* (smoked shoulder, served sliced) is something of a cult in Germany today. So what could be more natural than to smoke

Promoting progress in the Piedmont yellow pages.

and cook pork at the same time, by adopting the barbecue technique familiar from political and community events? And why barbecue the inferior parts of the hog when you can buy only the best part from your local butcher? Shoulders' fattiness meant that they didn't dry out and they absorbed even more of the delicious smoke flavor. That it was easier to transport them, to turn them, and to cook them evenly was a bonus. If you had a bad day at the stand, you had less left over. And if some folks wanted their meat sliced like pork roast, instead of pulled or chopped like old-fashioned barbecue— well, why not? Germans have always had a reputation for practicality and thriftiness.

Moreover, by 1900 the whole Piedmont was coming into its own. From Raleigh west and south to Charlotte, mills and factories were springing up, towns were becoming small cities, and the sort of go-getting, can-do, New South attitudes that a son of the Piedmont named W. J. Cash mocked in *The Mind of the South* (1940) were increasingly widespread. By contrast, as the Piedmont saw it, the East remained predominantly agricultural, conservative, opposed to progress. Maybe that went for their barbecue, too.

Why change? Because they thought it was an improvement, and didn't see any reason not to make it.

THE CAROLINA
CULTURE WARS

I said in the preface that people often disagree when it comes to barbecue. In North Carolina that's an understatement. Historically, East
Carolina and the Piedmont have differed about a great many things:
barbecue preferences are just one of the latest.

BY THE TIME of World War II, the distinctions between North Carolina's
Eastern and Piedmont styles of barbecue were well established and widely
understood within the state. The defenders of Eastern orthodoxy took pride
in doing it the old way (whole hog, with a vinegar and pepper sauce), Piedmont folks were equally proud of their new and improved product (pork
shoulder, with a little ketchup added to the sauce), and each region claimed
that its barbecue was better.

They still do. Many have learned the hard way that partisans can be fiercely
loyal to their local traditions. "You ought to see what happens when we write
about barbecue," says Kathleen Purvis of the *Charlotte Observer*. "That's when
I want to crawl in a trench and pull sheet metal over my head." Rosemary
Roberts, her journalistic sister at the *Greensboro News & Record*, agrees:
"Write about the succulent glories of Tar Heel barbecue at one's peril. It's
much safer to take on the National Rifle Association."

Fans of Eastern-style can be withering about the barbecue of their upstart
upland cousins. Usually they attack Piedmont barbecue for its heretical sauce.
As an Easterner who opened a "North Carolina Barbecue" establishment in
Maryland put it on a warning sign: "We Don't Hold with Tomatoes." "I've
never eaten red barbecue," Andy Stephenson of Stephenson's Bar-B-Q in

131

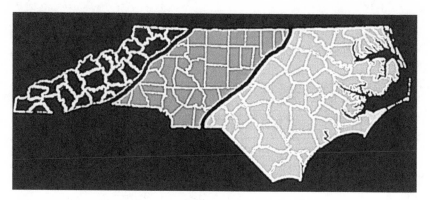

Eastern and Piedmont barbecue regions; mountains in the west.

Willow Spring told *USA Today*. "I've seen it, but that's as far as I care to go."
When the *Wilmington Star* devoted an editorial to sauce, it stated flatly that
"Proper Barbecue [is] basted with God's Own Sauce, whose ingredients include cider vinegar, red and black pepper, salt and maybe another thing or
two. But no tomatoes! That would make it the loathsome Lexington style."
Dennis Rogers of the *Raleigh News & Observer* concurred, pointing out that
"the Piedmont stuff is made with John Kerry's wife's ketchup vs. God's own
apple cider vinegar, salt and pepper Down East," and adding that "somebody
who would put ketchup on barbecue and give it to a child is capable of pretty
much anything." Jack Betts of the *Charlotte Observer* sounded like a peace-
maker when he remarked, "I like the eastern sauce myself, but don't regard
the western style as blasphemy worthy of a fist fight"—but then he added,
"A good western sauce can rescue a poorly-cooked pig."

As for those shoulders, Carroll Leggett dismisses what he sees as their
dreary "textural sameness," deploring the absence of "ribs, tenderloin, and
crispy skin"—"special parts to vie for" (even with the implication that there
are . . . other parts). Ayden's Pete Jones always maintained, "We smoke the
whole pig—if you don't use the whole pig, it's not barbecue," adding that "we
do a medium chop with some cracklin' added in there for taste and texture."
And Ed Mitchell of Wilson proudly proclaims himself "a whole hog cookin'
man, from the rooter to the tooter." If you "cut 'em up," he asserts, "you've
deviated from the real deal."

Piedmont partisans respond in kind. Jerry Bledsoe writes, "In the East,
you get all these little things in your mouth and wonder what the hell they
are. They're ground up pork skin. That's the only way they have to give the

meat any flavor." Peter Batke wonders about "people who would stuff a whole roast pig into a grinding machine snout first and douse the resulting detritus with pepper-speckled vinegar." Wayne Monk of Lexington Barbecue has observed, "As for 'whole hog,' there are some parts of the hog that I would just as soon not eat." And after Charles Kuralt criticized the shoulders at Statesville's Carolina Bar-B-Q as "too-refined, without the necessary grease and gristle" from whole-hog cooking, the management posted a notice next to the cash register that said "Extra Fat and Gristle on Request."

These arguments sometimes baffle outsiders. Georgian Bobby "Bobby Q" Cresap marvels, "You're talking about a little tomato being the basic difference between the two [Eastern and Piedmont], and they act like it's the Civil War." When Craig Claiborne, longtime food editor of the *New York Times*, paid our state a visit, he found the differences between Eastern and Piedmont "slight and subtle, the main one being the sauce ingredients. And even there, the absence of a tomato tang in the down east sauce didn't make a whole lot of difference—vinegar is the key factor in both of them. Shoulder vs. whole hog? Here again, not much to differentiate; in both cases the meat is cooked long enough to be fork tender."

Claiborne was a Mississippian, and modest enough to allow that the differences might be "obvious and pronounced [to] an experienced North Carolina barbecue addict." But even Bob Garner, who fits that description, observes that Piedmont barbecue is more like the Eastern variety than either is like what's called barbecue in Memphis, Austin, Kansas City, or Columbia. And Garner asks a good question: How can we expect outsiders to understand that we have the best barbecue in the country when we can't even agree among ourselves what good barbecue is? This sounds like a classic example of what Sigmund Freud called "the narcissism of small differences."

Jim Early of the North Carolina Barbecue Society once proposed a truce. "We've been shooting ourselves in the foot with this eastern-western thing," he argued. "No other states fight within the state. Let's stop that. Let's fight somebody else if we have to fight. Let's unite as kin." But when the *Atlanta Journal-Constitution* asked Jerry Bledsoe about Early's proposal, Bledsoe declined to hold his fire. "If this guy's trying to end the feud, I'm totally opposed," he said. "The feud is as good as the food."

Why can't we all just get along?

One reason may be that the barbecue battle lines are old ones. Low-level conflict between the East and the Piedmont has been going on since the 1700s. Over time the division has been cultural, economic, political, and demographic. The two regions were settled at different times by different peoples (two of them—English Episcopalians and Scotch-Irish Presbyterians—old adversaries). In antebellum times, different landscapes and resources meant that the fall line divided larger, wealthier, slaveholding farms in the East from smaller hardscrabble yeoman farms upcountry. The East had, and still has, a greater African American presence. And so forth. At the University of North Carolina this division was reproduced in miniature almost as soon as the university was founded. UNC students formed the Philanthropic Society in 1795 and the Dialectic Society soon after—literary and social clubs that quickly became regional, the latter for students from west of Chapel Hill, the former for those from the East. (Their fierce competition lasted for over a century and their colors, white and blue respectively, became the university's colors.)

This sort of intrastate division is not unusual: think of northern and southern California or Louisiana, or upstate New York and the city. Virginia's and South Carolina's divisions are quite similar to North Carolina's, having come about for many of the same reasons. But only in North Carolina, it seems, do different styles of barbecue correlate with these ancient fault lines. Only in North Carolina has barbecue come to symbolize the split and to serve as a badge of identity.

It is just barely possible that folks in the Piedmont started cooking pork shoulders with a ketchup-inflected sauce just to be different.

APPALACHIAN ANARCHY

Add to the now century-old difference between the barbecue styles of eastern North Carolina and the Piedmont an emergent "third way" in the mountains, and you may soon have a barbecue landscape almost as varied as that of South Carolina, where there are four distinct barbecue regions. As an out-of-stater I take no sides in this conflict, but I have to say that barbecue cooks in the North Carolina mountains can be awfully cocky for newcomers.

WHEN A NORTH CAROLINA conversation turns to barbecue, the mountain counties tend to get ignored. Indeed, when people speak of "western" barbecue they usually mean the Piedmont variety. This is because the state's Far West hasn't had much of a barbecue tradition until recently. Only two of the fifteen establishments in the Mountain region whose founding dates are given in Jim Early's *Best Tar Heel Barbecue* (2002) were in business before 1980, and none is older than the 1960s. Elsewhere in the state, half of the places Early discusses date from before 1970, and forty percent were cooking barbecue when Ike was in the White House.

This doesn't mean there's not good barbecued meat to be found west of Hickory—there's more of it all the time—but it does mean that barbecue places in the West aren't guided or constrained by any local tradition, and often look out-of-state for their models, especially since many cater to tourists and retirees and second-home owners whose idea of barbecue does not include North Carolina's thin vinegar-and-pepper sauces, or even necessarily pork.

So what you'll find in barbecue restaurants in the mountains is often
something more closely akin to the barbecue of Kansas City than to anything
served in Lexington or Goldsboro. Along with the pulled pork you'll usually
find ribs, not as one of the tastier results of whole-hog cooking, but bought
and cooked separately. (The Eastern and Piedmont attitude was summed up
by one Piedmonter who told the *Washington Post*, "If you want ribs, go to
a rib place.") You'll often find barbecued beef as well. And there'll probably
be a choice of sauces, usually including a heavy, sweet, tomato-based sauce,
similar to the bottled "barbecue sauce" introduced in the 1950s by Kraft
Foods, since widely imitated (and improved) and now found on grocery
store shelves and grilled burgers throughout the country. As Bob Garner
wrote disapprovingly in his classic *North Carolina Barbecue: Flavored by
Time* (1996), "You may find something *called* barbecue in some of the tourist destinations in the Smokies, but like the typical feathered, plains-Indian
headdress worn and sold in Cherokee, it isn't authentic to this state, but is
an import from the West."

Herb's Pit BBQ is a case in point. Nestled up against the Tennessee and
Georgia borders, Herb's is undoubtedly the westernmost barbecue restaurant
in the state. One of the oldest places in the mountains (founded in 1982),

Road sign for Herb's, on US Highway 64,
Murphy, North Carolina.

Herb's serves some good smoked meat, and they cook it with charcoal, which is rare everywhere these days. But their tasty pulled pork comes from loins and collars, not shoulders, and they serve ribs and beef as well. It's telling that the license plates on the wall are from Florida and New York.

In the hills you're also likely to encounter strange, non-canonical side dishes, like the garlic bread that comes with the barbecue platter at Fat Buddies in Franklin. And you're more likely to find names like "Fat Buddies"— most Piedmont and Eastern restaurants bear their owners' names.

In short, anything goes up yonder, encouraged by those out-of-staters who bring tastes and expectations from all over, have the money and inclination to eat out a lot, and don't see innovation and experimentation as uncalled for.

Food writer Jonathan Ammons echoed these observations in a 2014 article in Asheville's *Mountain Xpress*. He documented the "autonomous mountain barbecue scene" and a growing belief among its cooks that they're shaping a third North Carolina barbecue region, distinct from eastern North Carolina and the Piedmont.

"Mountain barbecue" in a 12 Bones cookbook.

If that's what's happening, though, it will be a region very different from the other two. Embodying a tradition of rejecting tradition, its style will embrace all styles. Asheville's 12 Bones Smokehouse, for instance, specializes in ribs, and they smoke a great many other things, including mushrooms. But none of it is *North Carolina barbecue* as heretofore understood. Co-owner Sabra Kelley observes that to cook Eastern- or Piedmont-style "there are definitely some rules that you have to follow," and she says, "We would rather be true to ourselves."

Their side dishes are also unconventional. It's "cool to see some place that doesn't just serve potato salad and coleslaw," a competing chef told Ammons. "And it can change every day!"—unlike "down South" (by which he seems to mean lowland North Carolina) where "people get pissed if they don't get their hushpuppies." The owner of Asheville's Bayou Bar-B-Q says, "People like different stuff up here; they don't want the norm"; his customers "want to try something that no one else has had."

This premium on innovation and willingness to cater to all sorts of customers can lead to a dizzying variety. At last count, Luella's, also in Asheville, offered eleven sauces, some traditional, some decidedly not—"a far cry," Ammons observes, "from the Eastern and Piedmont traditions of one true sauce, often chopped in with the meat."

All this innovation may indeed be becoming a tradition in its own right, as Lexington-style did a century ago. Keep an eye on it. North Carolina may soon have *three* competing, mutually scornful barbecue regions.

THE SPIRIT OF '66

★ ★ ★

Herewith, a history lesson from the Campaign for Real Barbecue. The proposed holiday has received vocal support from politicians of both parties, but so far, no action.

IN LATE FEBRUARY of 1766 the Royal Governor of North Carolina, William Tryon, attempted to win the good will of citizens who were growing restive under high-handed rule by treating them to a barbecue. He did not succeed: the New Hanover militia threw the barbecued ox in the river and poured out the beer. This was not an early expression of North Carolinians' preference for pork: they were upset about the Stamp Act.

Every schoolchild knows about the Boston Tea Party of 1773, when some rowdy New Englanders threw boxes of tea in Boston harbor to protest a British tax. Yet how many have heard of the Wilmington Barbecue?

Not only was it seven years earlier than the Tea Party, its story is much more colorful. While the Tea Party offers only a pitiful attempt to avoid the blame by dressing up as Mohawk Indians, the Barbecue involved a stand-off between the local militia and the British Navy, a conflict between the governor and the courts, a duel to the death, and a suicide by disembowelment. (The earliest known printed account can be found in Francois Xavier Martin's *History of North Carolina from the Earliest Period*, published in 1829, when the events would have been still—if just barely—within living memory.)

So why has the Tea Party had all the press? You need look no further than the title pages of American history textbooks. Until quite recently, nearly all of them were written and published in the Northeast. And the regional disparity in public relations skill persists to this day: Boston has a Tea Party museum entirely devoted to "the event that lead [*sic*] to an American Revolution!" while the Barbecue has been almost entirely forgotten, even in Wilmington.

We at the Campaign for Real Barbecue believe it is time to right this injustice. We have urged the North Carolina General Assembly to mark the anniversary of the historic events in Wilmington by declaring that the last Monday in February will be observed henceforth as "Wilmington Barbecue Day."

Striking a blow for liberty, 1766.

THE THIRD RAIL OF NORTH
CAROLINA POLITICS

The *New York Times* requested this piece and ran it the day before the 2016 North Carolina presidential primary. Full credit to the *Times* for realizing that their readers needed instruction. Yes, I failed to mention the two candidates who eventually ran against each other. (Full disclosure: the "snarky commentator" was me.)

HERBERT O'KEEFE, editor of the *Raleigh Times*, once said that "no man has ever been elected governor of North Carolina without eating more barbecue than was good for him." In our state the linkage between politics and barbecued meat dates back at least to 1766, when Royal Governor Tryon tried unsuccessfully to win the good will of citizens annoyed by the Stamp Act by laying on a barbecue in Wilmington. (It didn't work: The local Sons of Liberty poured out the beer and threw the barbecued ox in the river. Note that this was a full seven years before the Boston Tea Party, which gets all the publicity.)

In more recent times, barbecue has even figured as a campaign issue. When North Carolina's secretary of state Rufus Edmisten ran for governor in 1984, for instance, he got in trouble with an offhand remark. "I'd be eating barbecue three times a day for a solid year," he recalled, "and I got up one night and, in a very, very lax moment—the devil made me do it—I made a horrible statement. I said, 'I'm through with barbecue.' Well, you would have thought I had made a speech against my mother, against apple pie, cherry pie, the whole mess." He lost the election to a Republican (only the second one to be elected since Reconstruction).

A campaign derailed by barbecue.

In 2012 Michelle Obama also got burned by an ill-advised comment. When she announced that the Democratic National Convention would meet in Charlotte, she spoke of that city's charm, hospitality, diversity, "and, of course, great barbecue." Many Charlotteans were puzzled. A headline in the *Charlotte Observer* read, "Charlotte = great barbecue? Who knew?" Mayor Anthony Foxx said that his city has good barbecue, but not *great* barbecue: "I have had great barbecue in Charlotte that's been brought in on a truck." And one snarky commentator said, "Complete the sentence: As a barbecue town, Charlotte is, one, not what it used to be; two, like Minneapolis for gumbo; three, good enough for Yankees; four, not far from Shelby [home of Bridges Barbecue Lodge]."

But at least the First Lady meant well. You can't say that for Rick Perry. Shortly after the Texas governor announced in 2011 that he was running for president, the *Raleigh News & Observer* turned up an injudicious remark he'd made nearly twenty years earlier. In 1992 the same paper had reported that Perry, then Texas Commissioner of Agriculture, had eaten some eastern North Carolina barbecue and said he'd had roadkill that tasted better. At the time, some of us wondered why he had been eating roadkill, but we let it go. When a man wants to be president, however, it's a different matter. A typical response came from Jeffrey Weeks, in the *Charlotte Examiner*: "Rick Perry is not fit to be president of the United States. In fact, he is apparently not fit to be a guest in my house." The furor got national attention, and Perry withdrew from the race three months later. Surely not a coincidence.

North Carolina's primary is tomorrow and so far the subject hasn't come up, but it still could. If it does, my advice for aspiring politicians who aren't from around here is, watch what you say. If the subject is unavoidable, you'll get more respect if you're forthright in defense of your heritage. When Elizabeth Dole and Erskine Bowles were contending for the Senate in 2002, they were asked if they preferred the barbecue of eastern North Carolina or that of the Piedmont. Dole spoke for the style of her native Piedmont, but Bowles (who had criticized Dole for ducking tough issues) wouldn't say which he preferred—and he lost.

If obliged to say something about barbecue, you should, like Elizabeth Dole, stand by your place. When President Obama comes to North Carolina he eats ribs with a sweet, sticky, red sauce, and I don't think anyone holds that against him. Even though ribs barely count as barbecue in these parts, he's from Chicago, so that's what he *should* like. "I'm from Chicago and I'm a rib man" may be a sadly mistaken position, but it is not a contemptible one. Generally speaking, honesty is the best policy. So Bernie Sanders should say, "I'm from Vermont and don't know anything about it" and Ted Cruz, "I'm from Texas, so let's not discuss it."

If possible, though, try not to say anything. You're very likely to offend some North Carolina voters, and it's possible that you will offend them all. Just shut up and eat.

HOW HILLARY GOT SMOKED
IN NORTH CAROLINA

In the presidential election of 2016, North Carolina was supposed to be a "battleground state," but it wasn't even close. Donald Trump won handily, carrying seventy-six of the state's one hundred counties. This op-ed for the *Raleigh News & Observer* suggests one possible reason.

APPARENTLY national Democrats have heard that barbecue is a big deal in North Carolina, because when they come to our state they always make a point of eating it. But they usually get it wrong.

In 2000, for example, Al Gore knew enough to stop by a big political barbecue, but a friend of mine who was on the campaign bus says that when Gore got off the bus, he put his suit jacket *on*.

Just so, when Michelle Obama announced that the 2012 Democratic convention would be in Charlotte, she listed "great barbecue" as one of that city's attractions. But actually, Charlotte is an exception to the North Carolina rule. The *Charlotte Observer*, not usually averse to boosterism, published an editorial headlined, "Charlotte = great barbecue? Who knew?"

In 2016 Hillary Clinton continued this tradition of barbecultural cluelessness. It would have been so easy for her to visit, say, Wilber's Barbecue in Goldsboro. The owner, Wilber Shirley, is one of the last yellow-dog Democrats, a man who has a picture of FDR on the wall of his restaurant. There's a photograph on the web of him holding a Barack Obama bobblehead, "show[ing] the President around the smoke house."

Wilber had to settle for the bobblehead because the real Obama has never actually come to his place. The president prefers a place in Asheville that

Politician at the annual Mallard Creek Presbyterian barbecue.

Wilber Shirley shows President
Obama around his place.

serves ribs with blueberry-chipotle sauce. He probably does like ribs—he's from Chicago, after all—but trying to score barbecue points with North Carolina voters by eating ribs is like John Kerry's asking for Swiss cheese on his Philly cheesesteak, or Sargent Shriver's going to a tavern in an Ohio mill town and saying, "Make mine a Courvoisier!"

Mrs. Clinton didn't go to Wilber's either. She ate her barbecue at a place in Charlotte called the Midwood Smoke House.

Now, it's true that the food at Midwood is tasty, and its barbecued meats are cooked 100 percent with wood, which is commendable. But eating there is not the way to show voters that you're in touch with what one could call "deep" North Carolina.

First of all, it's in Charlotte. And to many North Carolinians "Charlotte" brings to mind not just barbecue that's less than great, but also big business, "gentlemen's clubs," and traffic jams. Charlotteans don't help when they suggest that the rest of us are—well, deplorables. (One *Observer* reader wrote, for instance, that "Charlotte has always suffered from an image problem, and it will only change when people separate 'North Carolina' and 'Charlotte' in their minds.") When Mayor Eddie Knox lost the 1984 Democratic gubernatorial primary, he may have been right to blame "the Mecklenburg [County] thing."

So, for starters, Hillary ate her barbecue in the wrong town. Moreover, she ate it at a trendy place in a trendy neighborhood, a place with an "executive chef," a bar that gets equal billing with its barbecue, and a menu offering not just pork barbecue, but also barbecued ribs, brisket, burnt ends, prime rib, ground chuck, sausage, chicken, and salmon, served with your choice of four different sauces.

You often find this indiscriminately omnivorous approach in places like Charlotte that are full of newcomers from many different barbecue traditions, or none, but it's not the Tar Heel Way. The one-true-faith North Carolina approach is exemplified by the Skylight Inn in Ayden, where Sam Jones says, "When you come here, it's not what you want, it's how much of it."

Yes, the Midwood is a barbecue place in North Carolina, but it's not a *North Carolina barbecue* place, and for all the political good it did her, Mrs. Clinton could have skipped the smoked meat altogether and gone to a tapas bar.

I'm sure that Donald Trump knows as little about North Carolina barbecue as Hillary does, but he got better advice. Somebody sent him to Stamey's in Greensboro, a venerable place that advertises its "Old Fashioned Barbecue." Somebody even told him to order chopped barbecue, sweet tea, hushpuppies, slaw, and cherry cobbler. He came away with a photograph, widely circulated, that showed him posing with the restaurant's staff, a fine, smiling cross section of North Carolina working people, pretty much the kind of folks who turned out on election day to put him over the top.

I'm not saying that Hillary could have won by eating at Stamey's, but would it have hurt?

Candidate Donald Trump at Stamey's, Greensboro.

TWO RECIPES

MOCK-RIDGEWOOD
BARBECUE SAUCE

East Tennessee doesn't have much of a barbecue restaurant tradition
(see pages 31–35), but it does have one famous barbecue restaurant,
cooking in its own idiosyncratic style and serving its barbecue with a
sweet, thick, red, and utterly delicious sauce. If you're going to use a
Kansas City-style sauce, this one is the one to use—even if it is from
Bluff City, Tennessee.

MIDWAY BETWEEN Johnson City and Bristol in upper East Tennessee,
not far from where my wife and I grew up in Kingsport, stands the small
town of Bluff City. Just outside the town is a barbecue joint known simply
as "the Ridgewood," a modest-looking place that since 1948 has served what
People magazine has called the best barbecue in the country—and therefore,
presumably, in the world.

But (I hear you say) what does *People* know about barbecue? OK, try this:
The Ridgewood is the only out-of-state establishment mentioned in Bob
Garner's book, *North Carolina Barbecue: Flavored by Time*. Given Tar Heel
chauvinism in these matters (largely justifiable), that is testimonial indeed.
Of course, Bluff City is only some twenty-five miles from the North Carolina
line, though nearly twice that far by mountain roads.

Folks drive a long way to eat at the Ridgewood for good pork (ham), well-
smoked, sliced very thin, and served with an incomparable sauce. In the old
days they went despite somewhat capricious hours and service that some
found brusque, even surly. (*Real Barbecue*, by Greg Johnson and Kingsport
boy Vince Staten, quoted one longtime customer who said that going to the

The Ridgewood, Bluff City, Tennessee.

Ridgewood was like going to the Don Rickles Restaurant.) But times have changed; these days the hours are regular and the service is the friendly sort you'd expect in East Tennessee.

I mentioned the sauce. Let me tell you about it. Like most sauces west of the mountains, the Ridgewood's is sweet, thick, and red. But the flavor is marvelously complex—what ketchup will taste like in heaven. This nectar is poured generously over the pork sandwiches before they are served, and there are squeeze bottles on the tables should you want some more. Naturally the recipe is a closely guarded secret, but a while back some ladies in Kingsport set out to duplicate it. Fred Sauceman, who literally wrote the book on the place (*The Proffitts of Ridgewood: An Appalachian Family's Life in Barbecue*), says he doesn't know the recipe, but he knows how many ingredients are in it and the ladies' recipe doesn't have enough. Nevertheless, I think it's a pretty good facsimile, and here it is:

INGREDIENTS:

24 oz. (weight) ketchup
¼ cup Worcestershire sauce
1 Tablespoon good prepared mustard
¼ cup cider vinegar
½ cup oil

5 Tablespoons white sugar
1 medium onion, finely chopped
1 large garlic clove, minced
3 Tablespoons molasses
1 Tablespoon Kitchen Bouquet
1 Tablespoon Tabasco sauce
salt and pepper to taste (start with ¼ tsp)

Mix these ingredients in a bowl, then blend the mix in a blender. Put the goop in a pot and heat it to the boiling point, then simmer it for 15–20 minutes. This recipe makes about a quart, and the sauce freezes well.

You probably don't want to baste with this, because the sugar in it makes it turn black and ugly looking (although it still tastes good). It makes a fine

Ridgewood sandwich, with Ridgewood sauce.

dipping sauce for ribs, and it's also great on beef brisket or chicken. Shoot, I've been known to eat it with a spoon. But it's best the way the Ridgewood serves it: just pour it on some barbecued pork, heaped on a big, warm, white-bread bun.

And if you're ever in upper East Tennessee, stop by the source and taste the original.

THE PIG PICKER:
A BARBECUE COCKTAIL

When I wrote a barbecue cookbook a while back, the recipes in the book were for traditional regional styles of barbecue, and for the traditional sauces, rubs, side dishes, and desserts that go with them. When the University of North Carolina Press asked for a recipe to put in their blog, however, I gave them one (not in the book) that could hardly be less traditional.

The toast I suggest was a favorite of my late pal Leonard "Slats" Cottrell, a proud Virginian. Its ambiguity makes it suitable for any company.

WE NORTH CAROLINIANS love our vinegar-based barbecue sauces. In fact, we love them so much we don't just splash them on barbecue: East of Raleigh we boil potatoes in sauce-spiked water; west of Raleigh sauce goes in the slaw dressing. So why not a cocktail with sauce in it?

Well, you got it. Amanda Fisher and Paul Bright, compilers of "The Great NC BBQ Map," have devised what they call the Southern Islander Shrub. A shrub, if you didn't know (I didn't), is a drink made with vinegar, sugar, and fruit; this drink mixes a vinegar-based North Carolina barbecue sauce, honey, and pineapple juice (that's the "Islander" part), and adds bourbon. Vinegar? Well, vinegar was introduced to barbecue as a substitute for harder-to-get lime or lemon juice. So think of this as a sort of whiskey sour, with some heat. Continuing the barbecue theme, Amanda and Paul serve their drink in a glass rimmed with smoked sea salt.

This recipe is really good, but my wife didn't much like pineapple juice, so I started fooling around with alternatives and came up with one that substitutes peach nectar. I also used cane sugar syrup instead of honey. Peaches and cane sugar make this drink even more Southern, don't you think?

Here's how to make what I call a Pig Picker.

FOR THE COCKTAIL

1½ ounces bourbon
1 teaspoon 2:1 cane sugar syrup
1 teaspoon peach nectar
1 teaspoon Eastern North Carolina–style barbecue sauce

FOR THE RIM

2:1 cane sugar syrup
Hickory smoked sea salt

Drizzle the syrup onto one half of a plate and pile some salt on the other half.
Rotate the rim of an old-fashioned glass in the syrup, then in the salt.
Add the four cocktail ingredients to the glass and stir.
Add a large cube of ice and drink, "To the liberation of our country."

2:1 CANE SUGAR SYRUP

Cane sugar is widely available, but if you can't find it,
use light brown sugar instead.

2 parts cane sugar
1 part water

Bring the water to a boil. Add the sugar and return to the boil, stirring. When the sugar has dissolved completely, remove from heat and let cool.

PEACH NECTAR

You can buy peach nectar, often in grocery stores' Mexican food section, but homemade is better.

4 cups peeled, sliced peaches (fresh or frozen)
4 cups water
½ cup sugar (or to taste)
1 Tablespoon lemon juice

Bring the peaches and the water to a boil, and boil for 5 minutes. Remove from heat and let cool. Blend in batches, then add sugar and lemon juice and stir well. This freezes well for future use.

BARBECUE SAUCE

I'm not taking sides in North Carolina's Eastern-Piedmont sauce wars, but for this purpose Eastern-style is better. It has more of a cayenne punch and you don't need the additional sweetness that Piedmont-style brings to the table.

1 pint cider vinegar
5 teaspoons crushed red pepper
1½ teaspoons kosher salt
1 teaspoon cayenne pepper
2 Tablespoons brown sugar

Mix the ingredients and let stand at least 4 hours.

HICKORY SMOKED SEA SALT

You can buy this or smoke your own or, for this purpose (don't tell anyone I told you this), you can add a couple of drops of "liquid smoke" to a half-cup or so of sea salt in a sealed container, shake it, and let it stand for a while. And it doesn't really have to be sea salt, either.

TO LEARN MORE

These are books that I have found particularly useful, plus two of my own. A couple are primarily guidebooks and a couple more are cookbooks, but most are histories, ethnographies, and appreciations.

Auchmutey, Jim. *Smokelore: A Short History of Barbecue in America*. University of Georgia Press, 2019.

Berry, Wes. *The Kentucky Barbecue Book*. University Press of Kentucky, 2015.

Elie, Lolis Eric. *Smokestack Lightning: Adventures in the Heart of Barbecue Country*. Ten Speed Press, 2005.

———, ed. *Cornbread Nation 2: The United States of Barbecue*. University of North Carolina Press, 2004.

Fertel, Rien. *The One True Barbecue: Fire, Smoke, and the Pitmasters Who Cook the Whole Hog*. Atria Books, 2017.

Garner, Bob. *Bob Garner's Book of Barbecue: North Carolina's Favorite Food*. Blair, 2012.

Goldwyn, Meathead. *Meathead: The Science of Great Barbecue and Grilling*. Houghton Mifflin Harcourt, 2016.

Haynes, Joseph R. *Virginia Barbecue: A History*. The History Press, 2016.

High, Lake. *A History of South Carolina Barbeque*. The History Press, 2013.

Johnson, Mark A. *An Irresistible History of Alabama Barbecue: From Wood Pit to White Sauce*. The History Press, 2017.

Meek, Craig David. *Memphis Barbecue: A Succulent History of Smoke, Sauce, and Soul*. The History Press, 2014.

Moss, Robert. *Barbecue: The History of an American Institution*, revised edition. University of Alabama Press, 2020.

Reed, John Shelton. *Barbecue: A Savor the South Cookbook*. University of North Carolina Press, 2016.

Reed, John Shelton, and Dale Volberg Reed, with William McKinney, *Holy Smoke: The Big Book of North Carolina Barbecue*, revised edition. University of North Carolina Press, 2016.

Staten, Vince, and Greg Johnson. *Real Barbecue: The Classic Barbecue Guide to the Best Joints Across the USA*. Globe Pequot, 2007.

Vaughn, Daniel. *The Prophets of Smoked Meat: A Journey through Texas Barbecue*. Anthony Bourdain Books / Ecco, 2013.

Walsh, Robb. *Legends of Texas Barbecue: Recipes and Recollections from the Pitmasters*, revised edition. Chronicle Books, 2016.

Worghul, Doug. *The Grand Barbecue: A Celebration of the History, Places, Personalities, and Techniques of Kansas City Barbecue*. Kansas City Star Books, 2001.

ACKNOWLEDGMENTS

Scot Danforth, director of the University of Tennessee Press, took a flyer on this book and I hope he doesn't live to regret it. His colleagues Jon Boggs and Kelly Gray were patient and usually accommodating with an author who knows he can sometimes be a pain.

Robert Elwood is the best indexer I've ever worked with. He came out of retirement to index this book and I thank him for it.

Many of these chapters have been published elsewhere. Thanks to the original publishers for letting me use them here. I'm also grateful to the people and institutions who let me use their photographs and drawings. Robert Moss provided so many that he should probably be acknowledged on the title page.

I thank Jim Auchmutey and Fred Sauceman for their comments and suggestions, and while I'm at it I thank Dan Levine and my other comrades at the Campaign for Real Barbecue, just because. Thanks to Linda Moore Miller for reading the manuscript, and for emotional support.

Finally, Dale Volberg Reed should get credit for photographs, research, and prose—but that's the least of what I'm indebted to her for.

SOURCES

"The History and Present State of Southern Barbecue," adapted from the introduction to *Barbecue: A* Savor the South *Cookbook*, by John Shelton Reed. Copyright © 2016 by the University of North Carolina Press. Used by permission of the publisher. www.uncpress.org.

"There's a Word for It: The Origins of 'Barbecue,'" *Southern Cultures* 13 (Winter 2007). Used by permission.

"Barbecue in the Heart of Dixie" was a review of Mark A. Johnson's *An Irresistible History of Alabama Barbecue*, published in the *Alabama Review* 71 (July 2018). Used by permission.

"Kentucky 'Cue" and "Does East Tennessee Have a Barbecue Tradition?" have not been previously published. Copyright © 2020 by John Shelton Reed.

"Barbecue and the Southern Psyche" was a review of Wilber "Pete" Caldwell's *Searching for the Dixie Barbecue: Journeys into the Southern Psyche*, published in *Southern Cultures* 13 (Summer 2007). Used by permission.

"Thank You for Smoking" originally appeared in *Chronicles: A Magazine of American Culture* (December 1988). Used by permission.

"Barbeculture in the 21st Century" is drawn from "Barbecue Sociology: The Meat of the Matter," in Lolis Eric Elie, ed., *Cornbread Nation 2: The United States of Barbecue*. Copyright © 2004 by the Southern Foodways Alliance. Used by permission of the University of North Carolina Press. www.uncpress.org.

"What Can Dwight Macdonald Tell Us about Barbecue?" was published as "Macdonald's Barbecue," *The American Conservative* (August 2019). Used by permission.

"You Call It Elevated, I Call It Hincty" has not been previously published. Copyright © 2020 by John Shelton Reed.

"Shall We Gather by the River?" was originally two columns published in *Chronicles: A Magazine of American Culture*, "Shall We Gather by the River?" (July 1992) and "Bubba-cue Judgment Day" (August 1992). Used by permission.

"Down South in East London" was published as "Queuing Up for Q in London's East End," *Southern Cultures* 11 (Fall 2005). Used by permission.

"The Campaign for Real Barbecue," guest post on Steven Raichlen's BarbecueBible.com (January 2018). Used by permission.

"What is Real Barbecue?" from the website of the Campaign for Real Barbecue, TrueCue.org.

"From *True 'Cue News*," taken from the archives at TrueCue.org/about.

"Busting a Barbecue Myth," from uncpressblog.com (6 April 2016). Used by permission of the University of North Carolina Press.

"BBQ & A," from BBQJew.com (March 10, 2009). Used by permission.

"The Piedmont Reformation," "Carolina Culture Wars," and "Appalachian Anarchy" are adapted from *Holy Smoke: The Big Book of North Carolina Barbecue*, revised edition, by John Shelton Reed and Dale Volberg Reed, with William McKinney. Copyright © 2008 and 2016 by the University of North Carolina Press. Used by permission of the publisher. www.uncpress.org.

"The Spirit of '66," adapted from "North Carolina Needs a New Holiday," uncpressblog .com (4 May 2016). Used by permission of the University of North Carolina Press.

"The Third Rail of North Carolina Politics," originally "The Politics of Barbecue," *New York Times* (4 March 2016). Used by permission.

"How Hillary Got Smoked in North Carolina," originally "How Hillary Tumbled into the NC Barbecue Pitfall," *Raleigh News & Observer* (7 December 2016). Used by permission.

"Mock-Ridgewood Barbecue Sauce," adapted from a chapter in Amy Rogers, ed., *Hungry for Home: Stories of Food from Across the Carolinas* (Charlotte: Novello Festival Press, 2003). Used by permission.

"The Pig Picker: A Barbecue Cocktail," uncpressblog.com (7 March 2016). Used by permission of the University of North Carolina Press.

ILLUSTRATION CREDITS

Uncredited illustrations are public domain or © DixiePix (Dale Volberg Reed).

ABOUT THE AUTHOR

John Shelton Reed's contributions to barbecultural studies include *Holy Smoke: The Big Book of North Carolina Barbecue* (written with his wife, Dale Volberg Reed) and *Barbecue: A* Savor the South *Cookbook*. He is cofounder and Éminence Grease of the Campaign for Real Barbecue (TrueCue.org).

"Me and Dale outside a funky place in Houston."

INDEX

North Carolina, 5, 6, 15, 16, 31, 34, 44,
52–53, 59, 97–98, 99, 111, 120–21,
123–48
*North Carolina Barbecue: Flavored by
Time* (Garner), 136, 151
North Carolina Barbecue Society, 133

Obama, Barack, 143, 145–47
Obama, Michelle, 142, 145
Ohio, 45
O'Keefe, Herbert, 141
Owensboro, KY, 8, **29**, 44, 53
Ozersky, Josh, 60, 76
Ozment, Gump, 25

Pennsylvania Dutch, 129
People (magazine), 151
Perry, David, 118
Perry, Rick, 142
Pie Fidelity (Brown), 74
Pig Picker, 156–57
Pihakis, Jim, 24
Pihakis, Nick, 24
Place Setting, The (Sauceman), 34
political campaigns and elections, 20, 32,
141–48
Pope, Alexander, 17
Porterfield, Robert, 32
Proffitts of Ridgewood, The (Sauceman),
152
Purvis, Kathleen, 60, 61–62, 65, 131

Quincy, Josiah, 20

Raleigh, Sir Walter, 15
Raskin, Hanna, 65
Real Barbecue (Johnson & Staten), **44**,
45–48, 151–52
Reed, Dale, 117–22
restaurants: Allen & Son (Chapel Hill,
NC), 43, 47, **48**, 60; Archibald's
(Northport, AL), 22; Arkansas Café

(London, England), 13, 50, 90–93,
91; Arthur Bryant's (Kansas City,
MO), 47; Auburn Avenue Rib Shack
(Atlanta, GA), 43, 47, **47**; Bayou Bar-
B-Q (Asheville, NC), 138; Beacon
Drive-In (Kingsport, TN), 33–34,
34; The Beast (Paris, France), 62–63;
Big Bob Gibson's (Decatur, AL), 22,
23; Big Chief Barbecue (Columbus,
GA), **39**; Bozo's Bar-B-Q (Mason,
TN), **58**; Brenda's (Montgomery,
AL), 22; Bridges Barbecue Lodge
(Shelby, NC), 52, **112**, 142; Broad
Street Barbecue (Kingsport, TN),
34–35; Brother Jack's (Knoxville,
TN), 43, 48; Buxton Hall Bar-B-Cue
(Asheville, NC), **61**, 63; Carolina
Country Kitchen (Brooklyn, NY),
13, 50; Charle's Vergo's Rendezvous
(Memphis, TN), **10**; Corky's
(Memphis, TN), **119**, 119–20; Daisy
May's (Manhattan, NY), 13; Deano's
Barbecue (Mocksville, NC), 59;
Dickey's (Chapel Hill, NC), 53, **53**,
64; Dixie BBQ (Johnson City, TN),
35; Dixie's (Bellevue, WA), 13; Dr.
BBQ (St. Petersburg, FL), 71, **72**;
Dreamland (Birmingham, AL), 53;
Dreamland (Tuscaloosa, AL), 22, **22**,
24, 53; E&W Barbecue (Kingsport,
TN), 33; Famous Dave's, **66**; Fat
Buddie's (Franklin, NC), 137; Golden
Rule (Irondale, AL), 22; Goode
Company (Houston, TX), 52, **52**; The
Granary (San Antonio, TX), **73**, 74;
Green Top (Dora, AL), 22; Harold's
(Atlanta, GA), 43, 47, **51**; Heirloom
Market (Atlanta, GA), 64; Herb's
Pit BBQ (Murphy, NC), 35, **136**,
136–37; Homegrown Smokehouse
& Deli (Portland, OR), 106; Homer
Hall's Dixie Pig Church of God Gate